# Mass Communication in China

Annenberg/Longman Communication Books
George Gerbner and Marsha Siefert, Editors
The Annenberg School of Communications
University of Pennsylvania

John Howkins

# Mass
# Communication
# in China

Longman
New York & London

**Mass Communication in China**

Longman Inc., 19 West 44th Street, New York, N.Y. 10036
Associated companies, branches, and representatives
throughout the world.

Copyright © 1982 by Longman Inc.

All rights reserved. No part of this publication may be
reproduced, stored in a retrieval system, or transmitted
in any form or by any means, electronic, mechanical,
photocopying, recording, or otherwise, without the prior
permission of the publisher.

Development Editor: Gordon T.R. Anderson
Editorial and Design Supervisor: Diane Perlmuth
Interior and Cover Design: Albert W. Cetta
Manufacturing and Production Supervisor: Anne Musso

.

The map of China on page vi first appeared in *Inter Media*, the
journal of the International Institute of Communications, and
is reprinted with permission.

**Library of Congress Cataloging in Publication Data**

Howkins, John, 1945–
  Mass communication in China.

  (The Annenberg communication series)
  Bibliography: p.
  Includes index.
  1. Mass media — China.  2. Mass media policy —
China.  3. Mass media — Political aspects — China.
I. Title.  II. Series.
P92.C5H58   302.2'3    81-8375
ISBN 0-582-28264-0    AACR2

Manufactured in the United States of America
9  8  7  6  5  4  3  2  1    82-5172

# Contents

*Foreword by Asa Briggs*   vii
*Preface*   xi
*Note on Sources*   xiii

1. China, Communism, and Communications   1
2. China Today: The Political Context   7
3. Broadcasting: Television and Radio   25
4. Film   65
5. Publishing and Printing   79
6. Telecommunications:
   From Beacon Fires to Satellites   95
7. Advertising   107
8. The Trade in Media Products   113
9. Signposts for the Future   119

*Appendixes*
A. A Chronology, 1900–1980   124
B. A Note on the Language   134
C. Population   139
D. Names and Addresses of Selected Media
   Organizations   141

*Bibliography*   148
*Index*   153

# Foreword

This pioneering study, based largely on first-hand evidence collected in China, is an interesting and important contribution to communications studies. By reason of its size, history and policies, China offers a very special case for analysis. Nonetheless, the analysis is fraught with many difficulties. While there never has been any want of slogans — communications are of vital importance to China's changing leadership — there has usually been a severe shortage of facts. The available statistics are unreliable, and in any event do not cover all the necessary range of indicators: no details are collected, for example, about audience research, and this must affect both domestic and foreign reactions. Mr. Howkins has assembled all that he can, but he has also supplemented and critically evaluated the main factors in the present situation by information collected in interviews and travels. His study is pioneering, therefore, not only by reason of its content but of his methodology: he has explored before he has analyzed.

His study should be of interest to at least four groups of readers — China specialists, a scattered group in different countries, many of whom observe what is happening from afar; communications scholars, for no comparative or international study of late twentieth-century communications policies can leave out China; students of Marx-Leninist options and strategies, for in China, at least, current communications policy is based on the premise that Marx-Leninist ideology by itself is not enough as a source of development programs; and general readers, for whom China continues to exert distinctive attractions.

In relation to the preoccupations of the first group, it is remarkable how often detailed studies of Chinese economic and political structures and processes leave communications out as a crucial factor, for, as Mr. Howkins points out, they affect communications both within governmental networks and between leaders and rank-and-files are a necessary ingredient both in administration and in agreement. He also discusses their role in relation to education and culture. The successful advancement of current policies clearly depends on the way in which the communications networks are managed—and improved. It is possible, moreover, in the age of satellites, which has always caught the imagination of the Chinese, to leap-frog some of the intermediate stages in the evolution of other countries' communications systems.

For communications scholars, even the bare chronology presented in this book is useful. Communications technology is the same in all countries, although the feasible social options are quite different. The organizational shells, however, are different also, and so, too, are the underlying philosophies, whether or not these provide an adequate underpinning for articulated communications policies. It is relevant to compare China with Canada in terms of size, with the Soviet Union in terms of history, and with the United States in terms of current policies. Mr. Howkins's monograph will need to be supplemented by further case studies, some of which are already being prepared under the auspices of the International Institute of Communications, before comprehensive and consistent comparisons can be drawn.

For students of Marx-Leninism, China will always provide a challenge. Even before the founding of the People's Republic, Chinese ways of approaching Marx-Leninist goals diverged from those in other countries following revolutionary paths, and since the foundation of the People's Republic in 1949 there have been richly contrasting — but always quintessentially Chinese — twists and turns of outlook and fortune. In this story, too, in which Shanghai as well as Beijing has always played a prominent part, arguments about communications have always had an important role. Lenin could emphasize the importance of electrification: in the post-1949 period the importance of electronics — and all that goes with and made it possible — is at least as important.

Fourthly, general readers will find it interesting to compare Chinese experience as set out in this study with their own. The study raises important general questions about the relationship between truth and propaganda, between the private and the public (not least with reference to communication by telephone and cable), and between bureaucracy and enterprise.

It is important to add that the study will be of value not only to *students* of systems — and their underlying theories — but to people concerned in business fashion with direct dealings with China. Two of the chapters deal with advertising, where there are new contacts between

China and outside, and with trade in media products. As far as the first is concerned, the controversial introduction of advertising represented not only a landmark in Chinese communications history but a source of new opportunities for non-Chinese enterprises. As far as the second is concerned, there is clearly a further opportunity for consortia activities. At the same time, misunderstandings are likely to arise because of the different characteristics of the Chinese social and cultural systems and all other social and cultural systems, both Eastern and Western.

There have been so many changes in China since the foundation of the People's Republic that it would require exceptional insight to determine whether or not there will be equally striking changes in the future. Every study of Chinese communications structures and policies, therefore, will have to go through several editions. This particular volume points the way.

Asa Briggs
*Worcester College, Oxford*

# Preface

In China, politics affects everything. The arrest of the Gang of Four in 1976 and, even more important, the battle for the leadership between Hua Guofeng and Deng Xiaoping, are not just political events in the Western sense of the word. They have marked in China a powerful desire for modernization in the best way the world can offer, with enormous impacts in the world's political, economic, industrial, and cultural arenas. For over ten years, China pursued the elusive target of ideological purity; "reds" took precedence over "experts"; foreign contacts were despised. Now the position is reversed. In October 1979, for instance, I sat talking with Zhao Ziyang, the impressive first party secretary of Sichuan who became prime minister the following year. He gave a most intelligent, well-informed comparative analysis of agricultural management in the UK, France, and China. Two years ago, it would hardly have been possible even to admit the possibility of alternatives to China's own methods.

Most of the interviews for this book were carried out during a visit to China in October/November 1979 at the invitation of the Ministry of Foreign Affairs, Beijing. I would like to thank the Ministry and the many officials throughout China (some of whom are listed below) who took the time, at an exceptionally busy period, to discuss China's communications media, and especially Feng Tsui and Cheng Shousan of the Ministry's Information Department who provided continuous guidance and support. I could not have visited China without the support of Nils Treving of Nord Media, to whom many thanks. I am most grateful to Brian Beedham of *The Economist*, and members of his group, for their friendship and assistance while in China. I also want to thank Christina Jansen, then of Beijing University, whose presence and contributions were important to me in so many ways.

# A Note on Sources

Information on China is very scarce. The bare necessities of government statistics, handbooks and reference books, national trade and professional associations, academic studies, consultants' reports, and market research have been and mostly still are unobtainable. Even telephone directories are hard to obtain, except for the slim *China Phone Book*, published by an enterprising couple in Hong Kong as a commercial venture; it's patchy but invaluable.

This book has drawn on three different kinds of sources. The most important are my interviews in China; they have been supported by official PRC announcements and by other published and nonpublished material in Europe and elsewhere.

The bulk of the interviews were carried out in Beijing; the remainder in Chengdu and Chongqing (Sichuan), and in Shanghai and Guangzhou. Most of the interviews were carried out by myself alone; sometimes with the help of Christina Jansen; while several were held with members of *The Economist* group. The interviews usually took place in offices of the people concerned; a few were held in my hotel. The meeting rooms were virtually identical, whether the interviewee was a deputy premier or a tele-communications engineer; but, of course, they varied greatly in size and splendor. The Chinese were consistent-ly very friendly and helpful and courteous although they could be as firm as a Westerner if they wished to stress one point or avoid another. The Chinese team usually consisted of two or three officials, and an interpreter, but one person would do most of the talking. Most meetings lasted for about one and one-half hours or longer.

There is very little indigenous written information in China, and the verbal interview is still the main means by which visitors can discover what is happening. It is not en-tirely satisfactory, because it is excessively formal. Our visitors' hunger for information of all kinds, and our tradi-tion of the free exchange of information, is almost as great a threat to current communist China as it was to the courtiers of imperial China, although there are signs that this secretiveness may be lessening. We are greedy for in-formation: for facts, opinions, gossip, comments. The Chinese are more hardheaded and more practical (espe-cially, of course, the Chinese the visitor tends to meet).

A further factor is that the Chinese have always taken their daily routine somewhat casually. *Beijing Review* once showed a picture of Zhou Enlai's diary for 4 January 1967, to demonstrate how busy he was. It was indeed a hectic period of crisis, at the beginning of the Cultural Rev-olution. Yet the prime minister worked only from 11 A.M. to about 6.30 P.M. For a Western politician it would seem like a holiday.

The main interviews in China were held with the following people:

Gu Mu, vice premier (member of the politburo; head of the State Capital Construction Commission, the Commission for the Management of Export-Import, and the Commission for the Management of Foreign Investments).

Chou Mu Chih, vice minister, Central Propaganda Committee, Central Committee Communist Party.

Yen Xiao Feng, vice minister, Ministry of Telecommunications.

Zhao Ziyang, first party secretary, Communist Party, Chengdu, Sichuan Province (member of the politburo; director, Revolutionary Committee, Sichuan); appointed prime minister in 1980.

Chen Hanbo, Chairman, Publishers Association of China.

Li Fang, director of administration, National Publishing Administration.

Lu, director of publications, State Publications Bureau.

Shen Liang, director of printing, State Publications Bureau (China Printing Corporation).

Jiang, technical manager, New China Printing Works.

Dao Wenhua, General Office, New China Printing Works.

Wu Peng, vice president, National Academy of Space Technology.

Xing Xilin, International Liaison Department, Central Broadcasting Administration.

Zhang Huashan, editor, Editorial Office, Central Broadcasting Administration.

Yi Xinhai, director, General TV Office, Central Broadcasting Administration.

Li Gouan, editor, Editorial Office, Central People's Broadcasting Station.

Zong Yimming, editor, Editorial Office, Radio International.

Xing Ying-chu, director, Beijing Radio Station.

Chang Yu-shen, vice director, Beijing TV Station.

Liu, vice director, General Office, Shanghai TV.

Cheng, vice director, Shanghai TV.

Yu Chiu-fan, manager, Western Europe Department, China National Publications Import Corporation.

Hong Zang, general director, China Film Corporation.

Wang Chuanshi, manager, Western Europe, China Film Corporation.

Shih Fangyu, vice director, Shanghai Film Studios.

Chou Manfang, actress, Shanghai Film Studios.

Gu Yuan Bing, director, General Office, Shanghai Fiber Optic Telecommunication System, Post Office.

Chen Yi Kuang, Chief Engineer, 519 Factory, Shanghai.

Li Chu Wen, vice director, No. 1 Sichuan Integrated Works for Printing and Dyeing, Cheng-tu, Sichuan.

Fang Jishi, vice chairman, Chu Qiao People's Commune, Cheng, Sichuan.

Yang, vice chief engineer, Zhong Qing Machine Tool Factory, Zhong Qing.

The second kind of information is the official announcement of state and party. The main source for these is the *Daily Bulletin* of the Xinhua News Agency (abbreviated here to XHNA), which provides an authoritative summary, ranging from 30,000 to 40,000 words, of the day's events in China and around the world.

The Xinhua News Agency (Xinhua means "New China") was founded on 1 April 1937 in Yanan and became the official news agency of the new People's Republic of China (PRC) in October 1949. It now has contacts throughout China, from the very highest elements in the state and party down to each commune. Its 130 foreign correspondents in 83 countries not only serve as journalists but have many responsibilities for China's propaganda and diplomatic activities. As well as the *Daily Bulletin* the agency publishes a daily newspaper called *Chankao Xiaoshi* ("Reference News") for internal distribution to party members, which has immense influence.

The second official PRC source is *Beijing Review*, a 32-page weekly magazine that provides a good general account of Chinese society and gives details of all the major state and party events.

The third category of information includes all published and nonpublished material that is generally available outside China. It ranges from the BBC's useful and authoritative monitoring reports (here abbreviated to Short Wave Broadcasts, or SWB, for the Far East) to books and articles that are considerably less reliable.

# Mass Communication in China

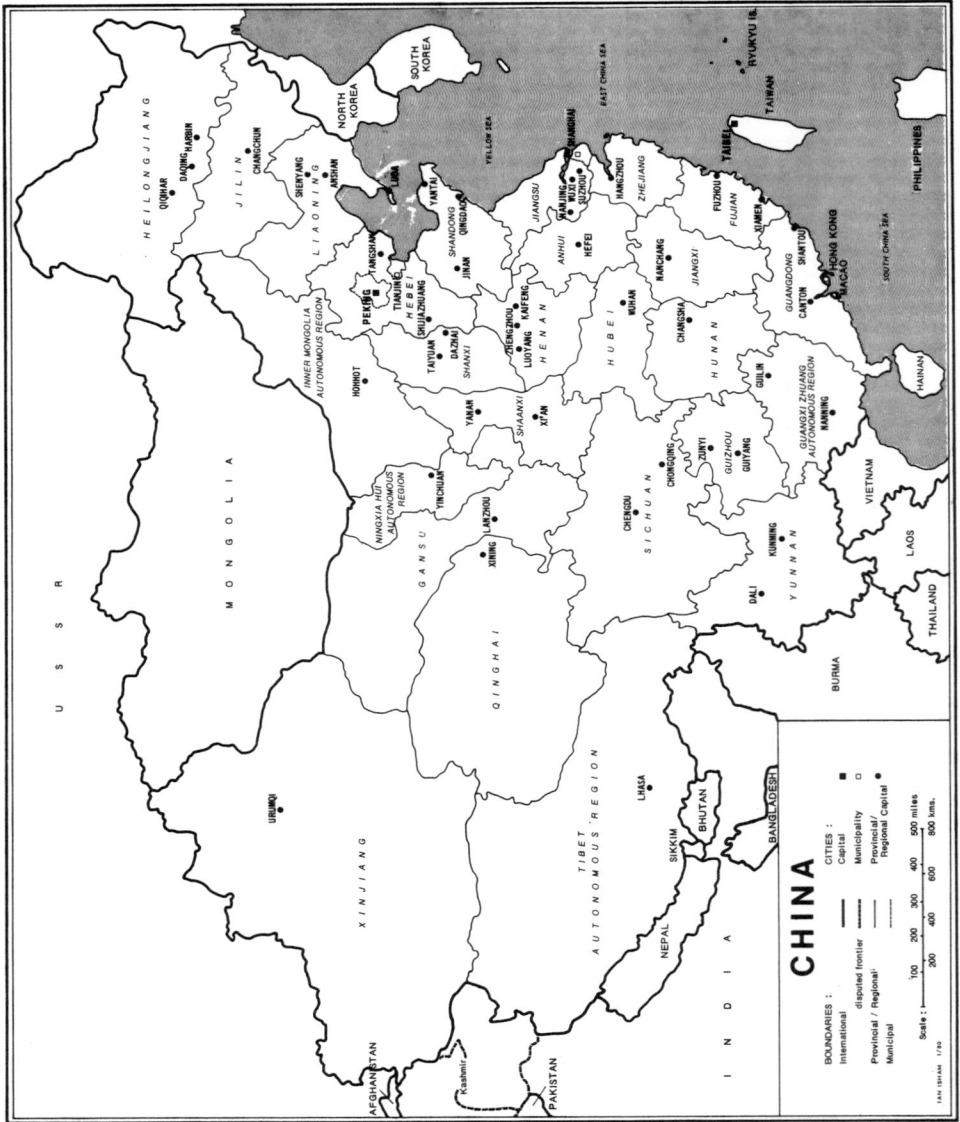

# CHINA

U S S R

MONGOLIA

HEILONGJIANG

QIQIHAR • DAQING •HARBIN

J I L I N

CHANGCHUN

L I A O N I N G

SHENYANG

ANSHAN

NORTH KOREA

SOUTH KOREA

YELLOW SEA

TANGSHAN
PEKING
TIANJIN
HEBEI
SHIJIAZHUANG

DAZHAI

TAIYUAN
SHANXI

YANAN

HOHHOT

INNER MONGOLIA
AUTONOMOUS REGION

NINGXIA HUI
AUTONOMOUS REGION

YINCHUAN

LANZHOU

XINING

G A N S U

QINGHAI

X I N J I A N G

URUMQI

T I B E T
A U T O N O M O U S   R E G I O N

LHASA

BHUTAN

NEPAL

SIKKIM

I N D I A

BANGLADESH

BURMA

Kashmir

AFGHANISTAN

PAKISTAN

JINAN
SHANDONG
QINGDAO
YANTAI

ZHENGZHOU
KAIFENG
LUOYANG
H E N A N

XI'AN
SHAANXI

JIANGSU
NANJING
WUXI
SUZHOU
SHANGHAI

ANHUI
HEFEI

HUBEI
WUHAN

ZHEJIANG
HANGZHOU

NANCHANG
JIANGXI

H U N A N
CHANGSHA

GUILIN

CHONGQING

S I C H U A N
CHENGDU

ZUNYI
GUIZHOU
GUIYANG

Y U N N A N
KUNMING
DALI

VIETNAM

LAOS

THAILAND

FUZHOU
FUJIAN
XIAMEN

GUANGDONG
CANTON
SHANTOU
HONG KONG
MACAO

GUANGXI ZHUANG
AUTONOMOUS REGION
NANNING

HAINAN

SOUTH CHINA SEA

EAST CHINA SEA

TAIBEI
TAIWAN

RYUKYU IS.

PHILIPPINES

BOUNDARIES :
International
disputed frontier
Provincial / Regional
Municipal

CITIES :
Capital
Municipality
Provincial /
Regional Capital

Scale :
100  200  300  400  500 miles
200  400  600  800 kms.

IAN IBHAM 1/80

# Chapter 1

# China, Communism, and Communications*

We are witnessing now the struggle of one of the world's oldest civilizations as it strives to modernize itself. China has unequalled problems and unequalled opportunities. In area, it is the world's third largest country, ranked only after the USSR and Canada (which is only slightly larger); with the USA being slightly smaller. It needs the land. It supports nearly one-quarter of the world's population; and has to feed them on the 11 percent of the land that can be cultivated.

China is very poor according to virtually all the economic indicators now in use. It is a rural, agricultural country. Its peasants number 800 million — nearly one-fifth

---

\* Parts of Chapter 1 and the chronology first appeared in *Inter-Media*, the Journal of the International Institute of Communications.

of the world population. Its gross national product is $424,620 million (1978); its income per capita is $460 (1978). Yet it has great assets: enormous mineral resources; a high growth rate; a huge and willing workforce, including many overseas Chinese who are skilled in finance and trade; a confident ideology; a sense of great responsibility; and, in large measure, the world's goodwill.

When I was in Beijing I quoted to my hosts in the Ministry of Foreign Affairs a remark by Sir George Staunton who accompanied Lord Macartney to China in the 1790s; the visit was Britain's first real attempt to establish diplomatic relations with the Qing (or any other dynasty). Sir George had written that "China is the grandest collective object that can be presented for human contemplation and research." My hosts smiled and answered, "for human activity too."

There is a long tradition of foreigners going to China and getting it wrong, and in the 30-odd years since Liberation the opportunities for getting it wrong have multiplied exponentially. The traffic is still dominated by China scholars working from the outside in, instead of from the inside out. This kind of sinology is exemplified in one recent collection of essays, *The China Difference*, edited by Ross Terrill, which feels it has to repeat the truism that "China and America are different." Couve de Murville, the former prime minister of France, was being equally bland, if for reasons of politic caution, when he returned from China in 1972 to report that China was "big and old."

China's own perceptions of itself often puzzle the visitor. The student of communications has especial problems. The Chinese do not have concepts or words to match the West's common coinage of communications, information, media, and so on. When pressed, of course, even the Westerner may have difficulty in defining these notions, an act of failure, even abnegation, which greatly surprises the Chinese, who tend to know what they mean. Nor do the Chinese have much time for the spirit of "independent inquiry" in which many current academics visit China.

What is the spirit of China is difficult to grasp. For instance, the Chinese will repeat how "backward" is Chinese society and technology, yet proudly accept in global organizations a financial commitment which is not at all that of a poor backward country but rather that of a great world leader. To the Chinese, of course, China is a great world leader which happens to be backward at this moment through the depredations of imperialism, nationalism, civil war, invasions and, closer to home, the Gang of Four. The pride of simplicity, the strength of simplicity, and the strength of pride are keys to China today.

The duality is often seen in China's work on new technologies—new, that is, to all societies. A senior delegation from the American Institute of Aeronautics and Astronautics recently visited some Chinese factories of space technology. They were impressed. China was competitive with U.S. systems in space transportation and the infrared technology that is vital for military and remote sensing. The delegation's leader reported that "the Chinese are serious about their stated goal of obtaining an independent capability in communications satellites in this decade and are making good technological progress towards it." His conclusion was percipient: "Their own frequently cited description of their technology as 'primitive' is excessively modest. Advanced but simple is more apt."

Advanced, and not always simple. In the last few years two British companies have tried to sell to the Chinese some automated typesetting machines capable of handling Chinese characters. One machine, developed at Cambridge University and marketed by Cable and Wireless, was simple and cheap (a minimum of £10,000). The other, by Monotype, is complicated and costs a minimum of £120,000. The Chinese favored the latter, and spent some £500,000 on installations in Beijing and Shanghai. Cable and Wireless did not manage to sell a single version of their machine to the Chinese, and have now withdrawn it.

In all countries the links between communications (roads, TV, handshakes) and society are multitudinous. It is sometimes suggested that a society exists to the extent that it communicates. In the USA and Japan, where information is becoming the dominant economic product and creator of wealth, a new kind of "information society" is said to be replacing the old "industrial society."

In China, communications and society are matched to a greater degree than anywhere else. Truly, communications *is* society. Two factors are significant here. First, communications and the media are, simply, very important to China and are likely to become even more important in the future. Second, however, the Chinese regard communications very differently than do other societies.

All armies depend on communications, and guerrilla armies especially so. In its initial years during the civil wars (the twenties and thirties) and during the war with Japan (1937–1945), the Chinese Communist Party required communications to survive, and they knew that good communications would assist them greatly to victory. At Liberation (1949), communications became even more important. The CCP was faced not only with establishing its government in one of the world's largest and most fragmented countries, devastated by years of fighting, but also with gaining the support of a people many of whom were either indifferent or hostile. Fortunately, Mao Tsetung and others were aware of the problem and had prepared for its solution. Their strategy was wholly innovative. They used communications in ways and to a degree never before imagined. Several Chinese writers (notably Godwin Chu, see bibliography) have examined the CCP's use of social pressure, of consensus, of ideological indoctrination, of teaching, of correct thinking.

The agent of communications was and is the CCP. The CCP is one of the most democratic political organizations in the world. It is not democratic in terms of its electoral routines, which are minimal (although in the local congress elections of December 1979 there were, for the first time, more candidates than posts), or its intolerance of dissent. But it can claim to be exceptionally democratic in terms of the involvement of its members at all levels, and in the formulation and execution of policy. In 1949, therefore, the CCP was able to use itself as a communications medium, a real mass medium. It remains an astonishing achievement.

In China today, the main medium of communications is not broadcasting or newspapers or the cinema, but the CCP. The main resources of communications are not wavelengths or printing presses but party members (about 38 million people, some 4 percent of the population). The cadres' main tools are not TV programs but discussions.

This interpretation of communications explains the dominant role of the "dazibao," the posters which, both on Democracy Wall, and in the villages, have played such an important part in Chinese society.

It's interesting, in this light, that the logo of *Renmin Ribao* ("People's Daily"), the main national newspaper, is written in Mao's own script. The characters have not been altered in the recent troubles. However, Mao's characters denoting the Bank of China that have long embellished its branch in Singapore have not been so lucky. They were replaced in September 1979 by new characters reputed to be by Hua Guofeng.

China's attitudes to communications and media are

very closely linked to the people's awareness of their importance. The same character has always been used to indicate both the mass media and publicity and propaganda. The Chinese also use the same character for literature and civil power.

Consider the analogy of China as a mammoth conglomerate, China Co. Ltd., and imagine that China Co. Ltd. is offered a sophisticated, expensive printing press that will enable the company newspaper to be printed a few hours faster. In a market economy, a few hours might be worth a great deal of money; deadlines are pushed back, and the publishing schedule becomes less sensitive to strikes and disruptions. The paper would be commercially much more competitive. But in China there's no competition; why spend money to produce the house journal a few hours earlier? The clash between this traditional totalitarian system and the protagonists of modernization is one of the motifs of China today.

# Chapter 2

# China Today: The Political Context

China is very old, but the history of the People's Republic of China is very short. It celebrated its thirtieth birthday on 1 October 1979. The Chinese think, act, and work in the context of those last 30 years, and the next three.

The new republic saw great changes. In 1949, Liberation from a corrupt, nationalist government to a communist democracy; then, the Great Leap Forward (1958), followed by two steps backward and Russia's withdrawal of her support for the new China. In 1966 China embarked on the Cultural Revolution, led by Mao Tsetung, one of the world's fiercest, most complicated, and most perplexing events, which was more like a civil war than a revolution and which, even now, remains a conundrum. Slowly, the country withdrew into itself. China closed its doors.

It was ten years before China decided that isolation

was the wrong policy. The decision was a hard one, but probably inevitable. China is a large country (the world's largest population in the third largest area): more important, perhaps, are her great ambitions and her skills. The Chinese Communist Party has always had some intriguing, even unique, ideas about development. In a world that is increasingly interdependent, China could not but become increasingly aware of others (and others of China) and aware, too, of the need to communicate with others, to exchange information. The first priority would be the apparently neutral matter of technology. But it would not be long before the Chinese were willing to talk about ideas, theories, methods, of agricultural production, of marketing, of workers' incentives, even of capitalism and profit sharing.

China's decision to open the doors again, and her manner of doing it, was inextricably linked to the confusion of the early seventies and to the deaths in 1976 of Zhou Enlai and Mao Tsetung. The chronology is complicated; interpretation is hazardous. At the time, ignorance and confusion were endemic, and hardly distinguishable. Nobody got near to predicting the rise of Hua Guofeng, nor the rise, fall, and rise again of Deng Xiaoping. Yet a grasp of these events is crucial to an understanding of how China sees itself and how it works.

We need some classifications, some labels, to make sense of the opposing camps. The West's favorite division into right-wing and left-wing is useless (Jiang Qing, Mao's widow, was generally described as ultra leftist during the Cultural Revolution and as ultra rightist after it). But one of Mao's own phrases, which provided a key theme of the Cultural Revolution in the media and elsewhere, is the dichotomy between "red" and "expert." Put simply, the choice facing the Chinese in the Cultural Revolution, and a major issue today, is the choice between ideology and expertise, between the radicals and the moderates, between pure politics and pragmatism, between time given to political education and self-education and time given to work in the fields or in the factories, between promoting those who are ideologically correct and those who are good at their jobs, between keeping one's eyes fixed on Mao and looking aside to what foreigners have to offer, between class struggle, in which all privileges must be abolished, and commercial competition in which bonuses and perks can substantially increase a worker's wages. The Cultural Revolution was a great cleansing of China, in which the "reds" dominated politics, the economy, all cultural matters, all life. In 1978, the experts regained the helm. Modern China is a tension between the two forces. This tension must be understood.

The current chapter in the story starts back in 1973, when Deng Xiaoping, who had been purged in 1967 during the most extreme, the "purest," months of the Cultural Revolution, was rehabilitated and made a vice premier. China generally has about a dozen vice premiers, most of whom, but not all, are on the all-important political bureau (the politburo) of the Central Committee of the Chinese Communist Party (CCP). Deng's protector was Zhou Enlai, the grand old man of China, who had been elected premier in 1949 and still held the post in 1973. Both Zhou and Deng were keen to push for China's modernization, and for economic and technological growth; both preferred people who were capable ("expert") over those who were politically pure ("red"). Throughout 1974 Deng consolidated his position. In 1975 the party held its Fourth National Party Congress, which is its supreme organ and would elect the Central Committee. Zhou was now seriously ill but he managed to dominate the NPC (largely from his sickbed) and to ensure that Deng was made vice chairman of the Central Committee and chief of staff of the People's Liberation Army — and heir apparent to Mao. The experts appeared to be ascendant. The following year, however, on 8 January, Zhou Enlai died.

At the start of 1976, therefore, the moderates had just been bolstered by some recent success, but they lost their protector. Mao, the greatest figure in the history of the republic, and the protector of the reds, continued to live, although gravely ill, for eight more months. Those eight months were crucial.

As January turned into February there emerged a bitter rivalry between Deng and Mao, between the moderates and the militants. The chairman, by now, was very ill; but his power and influence was exploited to the utmost by Jiang Qing and the Gang of Four, and by the cohorts of party members who owed their careers and power to the Gang's (and Mao's) success in the Cultural Revolution and later. It is worthwhile describing the Gang of Four in some detail. Many Westerners find the continual reference to the Gang as being crude, if not naive, and extraordinarily vindictive. They dislike slogans, they regard this one as unnecessary, and they are embarrassed. Yet it is true that the Gang of Four have been referred to constantly from the moment of their arrest until their trial in 1980–1981, when the emphasis changed. By the time of the trial, moreover, the cohesion of the Gang had weakened. In November 1980 the more usual description of the Gang of Four and their associates was the "Lin Biao and Jiang Qing cliques." Why this prominence?

The members of the Gang of Four share the two crucial experiences of having lived and worked in Shanghai, and of having come to power through the Cultural Revolution. The best known is Jiang Qing, Mao's widow. Jiang grew up in Shanghai (under her real name, Lan Pin) and was an occasional film actress at the famous Shanghai

Film Studios. I was told by her former colleagues at the studios that she never rose above a very lowly grade. But she was lively, attractive, and ambitious and by the mid-thirties she had become a close friend of Mao Tsetung, then embroiled in party factions. When the pair married in 1940, Mao's fellow leaders insisted that his new wife should take no part in party politics and discussions. Mao agreed, and for over twenty years Jiang stayed in the background. The turning point came in the mid-sixties when Mao put her in charge of the Beijing Opera, with some unstated responsibilities for guiding the country's cultural life. She responded, with vigor, and as Mao grew older she began to enjoy an increasing influence first on the politics of culture and then on the national government. She was already powerful by the time of the Cultural Revolution.

The main battle lines of the Cultural Revolution were crystallized in 1965 in several articles by Yao Wenyuan, the Gang of Four's chief theoretician. Yao's most famous piece attacked a play written by the deputy mayor of Beijing; both the play and Yao's criticisms of it were explicit allegories of the state of the nation; more particularly, the way Mao was running the country. Yao's articles continued to be signposts in Mao's campaign and he eventually became a vice chairman of the party.

Many of Yao's articles were published by Zhang Chunqiao, the third member of the Gang of Four. Zhang had been a senior official in the Xinhua News Agency and in 1967 became chairman of Shanghai's Revolutionary Committee. He is generally regarded as the most intelligent and statesmanlike of the four and the man who was destined, according to the plan, to be prime minister. The fourth member of the Gang was Wang Hongwen, who fits the image of the Red Guards so popular in the West; raucous in speech, violent in temperament, dashing, practical, and enthusiastic. He rose to become a vice chairman of the party in 1973 but then made the great mistake of directly challenging Zhou Enlai, whereupon he was forced back to Shanghai.

The reason for the Gang's fame, both in success and failure, lies deep in the psychology of Chinese politics and manners. If a leader is successful, his success is due to his intimate involvement, if not identity, with the masses; therefore, it would be invidious to single him out. It is permissible to quote a leader's remarks, but nothing else is personalized. However, if a leader fails, or is incorrect, his failure is due to his betrayal of the masses. In fact, he stops being one of the masses. Therefore, he regains individuality and can be named. There is also the natural desire to blame someone for the awful years of the Cultural Revolution and afterwards.

To return to the days following the death of Zhou. Deng and the moderates faced the powerful combination of Mao (nearing his dotage), the Gang of Four, and the militants. The prize was the government of China. Deng lost. On 8 February, Xinhua News Agency announced that a vice premier called Hua Guofeng, currently minister of Public Security, had been appointed acting premier. He had come to Beijing in 1971. He had got on well with both Mao and Zhou and was appointed a vice premier in 1975. He was relatively young (56 years old, which is very young for a Chinese leader) and relatively unknown.

In early April there took place in Beijing one of those spontaneous demonstrations of political fervor, of personal loyalty, which in China (and not only in China) often mark major shifts in the country's political stance and indicate that new aims, new directions, are being sought. On 3 and 4 April (a major feast day for the celebration of ancestors) huge crowds gathered in Tienanmen in Beijing to pay their respects to the late Zhou Enlai. Tienanmen is the vast square that lies at the center of Beijing, of the republic itself. It is bounded, to the north, by the Tienanmen gate, the entrance to the Forbidden City, on whose balcony Mao proclaimed the new republic on 1 October 1949. It is also the site of the Great Hall of the People, where the National People's Congress meets, and of the national museums. It echoes Red Square in Moscow; but Tienanmen is both more ancient and more alive.

The crowds that gathered to lay wreaths and memorials did so in such a way that their remembrances of Zhou were clearly seen as symbolizing support for Deng, the old man's protegé, and for the program of modernization and good management that they, and others, had started to introduce. They marked, also, a desire to be rid of the rigors and ideological traumas of the Cultural Revolution and a desire for moderate, sensible, practical government. It was a massive plea for moderation.

But Deng and the moderates could not capitalize on this display of support. The radicals acted faster. The wreaths were removed, there were riots, many demonstrators were arrested. The Gang of Four, who were in practical control of the government (Mao stopped receiving visitors in June), ensured that Hua was made first vice chairman of the party and that Deng, who had been criticized slightly since Zhou's death, was publicly condemned. But the Tienanmen riots had indicated a feeling in the country that could not be so easily capped, and the victory of the Gang of Four was short lived.

On 9 September, Mao Tsetung died. As Zhou's death took the leader of the moderates, so Mao's death took away the leader of the radicals. The way to compromise was open. Hua quickly emerged as a much stronger and astute person than had been thought. Less than a month after Mao's death, on 6 October, Hua sent Mao's former bodyguard and a picked team of men (known as unit

8341) to arrest the Gang of Four. The following day Hua was named by the politburo to be chairman of the party and chairman of the important Military Commission of the PLA. Over the winter, he consolidated his position still further.

In April 1977 large crowds gathered again in Tienanmen to honor Zhou and his ideas and, once again, to indicate their support for Deng. The masses' desire for moderation and calm were evident; and, this time, there was no Gang of Four to counterattack. The question of Deng's rehabilitation was uppermost in everyone's minds.

The Political Committee that purged Deng in February 1976 was not much different in membership from the committee that welcomed him back in the spring of the following year. But welcome him back they did. By July Deng was back in the Political Committee and working as deputy premier and chief of staff of the PLA. The task was awkward; it required a complete volteface; yet it was done. It was another revealing insight into how, in China, a consensus can change from one extreme to another in a moment of time.

The changes had immediate effect. In March the government lifted its ban on the playing of Beethoven's music; in May, on Shakespeare's writings. Even more symbolic was the holding in Taching of the National Industrial Conference, with some 10,000 delegates. It was the first to be called since 1949. China was set fair on the road to modernization.

The years 1977 and 1978 were years of consolidation. The country was emerging (is still emerging) slowly but surely from ten years of civil war, not a war of the military (although fighting took place in many places), but a war of slogans, of ideology, of ideas; a war of nerves. Everyone had to reconstruct his or her own state of mind and then start to repair the country after the depredations of the Gang of Four. The most common description of the effects of the Gang of Four is "sabotage"; the title of a leading magazine is *China Reconstructs*. After a crisis, individuals can appear to recover fairly quickly, while factories, mines, the land, machines, distribution networks, banking systems, take much longer. Nevertheless, as Gu Mu, vice premier, said in October 1979, "The low level of management and cadres (party officials) is an outstanding problem in the modernization program."

During 1977–1978 the new government, with the support of most of the masses, wholeheartedly pursued the path of economic expansion and modernization. The main slogan was the four modernizations of agriculture, science and technology, industry, and national defense (first enunciated by Deng in 1973 and picked up by Hua in 1977). The watchword was practicality. Unfortunately, they went too far, too fast. In March 1979 Deng had to apply the brakes to his own momentum. He managed to stop some of the more liberal measures without, it appears, losing any popular support.

The new policies were announced in 1979 at the second session of the Fifth National People's Congress (each congress lasts for five years and holds one session in each of those five years). Hua's report at the session on the work of the government is a major document in the new regime. Its tone is clear from a remark, towards the beginning, that "Our press, broadcasting, television, and publications are developing in a lively manner." Hua is quite right and, as in so many other countries, the Chinese media provide a touchstone of the country's health.

It is worth quoting from the report at some length. Hua was not speaking as a Western politician might speak. He is more like the chairman of the board (with Deng as chief executive officer, perhaps) of the largest conglomerate in the world: China Co. Ltd. His remarks, clearly made with Deng's support, are policies-as-orders. The key of the report was modernization: "Class struggle is no longer the principal contradiction in our society; in waging it we must center around and serve the central task of socialist modernization." But Hua admitted that the policies of the four modernizations had not gone as well as they should: "Some of the measures we adopted were not sufficiently prudent . . . coordination within and between industrial departments [i.e., the various sectors of the company] is lacking in many respects. In capital construction, far too many projects are being undertaken at the same time and many will not contribute to our production capacity for years." In summary: the last year was too ambitious; we misjudged priorities; we were not as efficient as we could be and as we have to be.

Said Hua, "We should therefore devote the three years beginning from 1979 to readjusting, restructuring, consolidating, and improving the national economy. This is the first battle for the four modernizations. To modernize agriculture, industry, national defense, and science and technology in a big country like China with over 900 million people [probably nearer 1000 million] is a highly complex and difficult task. Hence, further strengthening of the groundwork is an important precondition for smooth development later."

Hua's report at the second session, and the speeches of his colleagues on the Central Committee provide a thorough and detailed plan for action. The hallmark is practicality. The session acknowledged that Marxism-Leninism-Mao Tsetung Thought (the clumsy term for the party's ideology) is not a sufficient basis for solving the problems that now face China. Other ideas, theories, and models are needed.

Television provides a current example. The provincial capital of Shanghai has several TV and radio factories. The municipality of Shanghai (and the central government in Beijing) is now faced with a series of decisions of production, distribution, prices, discounts, and so forth, that are entirely novel. Shanghai would like to sell most of its TV sets to its own people. Is this legitimate? Should it be allowed to offer discounts? Should it concentrate on color sets that can receive Shanghai's own color transmissions or on black and white sets that are much cheaper and more popular with the large majority of Chinese who are not within range of a color signal? Should TV carry advertisements? Should the Shanghai municipality assist towns that are outside its own borders to get TV sets, construct relay transmitters, and so receive its programs? Does it then have a duty to serve these extraterritorial audiences with programs about their locality at the expense of programs about Shanghai itself? Where can answers be found?

In the USA, the communications industries are regulated by a law that was passed in 1934, before television really started and before anyone had even thought of satellites. In China, they are working on the basis of political philosophies, Marxism-Leninism-Mao Tsetung Thought, that make the 1934 Communications Act seem a model of useful regulation. In China, furthermore, they do not have an agency with the skills and experience of the Federal Communications Commission, which, however much it might be critized, does provide a most useful platform for the formulation of policy.

Clearly, other criteria than Marxism-Leninism-Mao Tsetung Thought are urgently required if China is to fulfill its own new goals of modernization. The second session of Congress went a long way towards saying that industrial enterprises should have more power to make their own decisions about capital investment, labor, prices, and so on. Also, that provinces, municipalities, and towns should have more autonomy vis-a-vis Beijing. The notion of "marketing" was raised and applauded; measures should be taken to "correct the dislocations between supply, production, and marketing."

The importance of importing technology was heavily stressed: "In three years, by learning from foreign countries, importing technology, and exerting our own efforts in innovation and enterprises, we should enable a number of enterprises in the main branches of the economy to adopt the world's advanced technology and employ it in key areas of production." The process of learning from abroad started in 1977, of course: it shows no sign of diminishing, although the priorities change continuously. At the second session, said Hua, "Economic exchanges between countries and the import of technology are indispensable, major means by which countries develop their economy and technology."

He continued: "Each enterprise should have a leading body [i.e., a board of management] which includes technical experts. Enterprises should encourage technological innovation, develop scientific research, and, provided it meets practical needs, adopt advanced technology in production and management to the greatest extent possible."

The state of China's economy can be roughly gauged from the information given on annual and longer-term plans. The 1978 budget was nearly but not quite balanced. Revenues totaled 112,111 million yuan and expenditures totaled 111,093 yuan — a surplus of 1018 million yuan.

The draft budget for 1979 was set to balance income and expenditure at 112,000 million yuan. The closeness of the 1979 and 1978 figures, after the rapid rise of the previous year, expressed the leadership's concern about going too far, too fast. The main priority was still agriculture but special priorities were given to light industries, fuel and power, building materials, transport, and communications. Also, said Hua, "The electronics industry has an important role to play in modernization and therefore must be vigorously developed."

The final figures actually recorded a deficit of about 16 million yuan, which was financed by 8 million yuan of carried forward surplus and a 9 billion yuan overdraft from the Bank of China (as announced by Wang Bingqian, Minister of Finance, at the third session of the Fifth National People's Congress, 30 August 1980). Revenues were down slightly at 11,033 billion yuan. See table 2.1.

**Table 2.1**  National Revenues, 1979/80

|                        | 1979 actual (billion yuan) | 1980 estimated (billion yuan) |
|------------------------|---------------------------|-------------------------------|
| Industrial enterprises | 49.29                     | 46.06                         |
| Taxes                  | 53.78                     | 54.4                          |
| Foreign loans          | 3.53                      | 3.39                          |
| Depreciation funds     | 2.46                      | 2.2                           |
| Other revenues         | .65                       | .24                           |

The cause of the deficit was the unexpectedly high expenditures of 127.39 billion yuan, of which 7.09 was taken from foreign loans for capital construction, and the remainder (120.30) as shown in table 2.2.

The draft 1980 budget set the state's revenues at 106.29 billion yuan and expenditures at 114.29 billion yuan, the deficit to be financed by a further loan from the Bank of China. The budget for 1981, which is the first year of the sixth Five Year Plan, set revenues at 115.46 billion yuan and expenditures of 120.46 billion yuan, a deficit of 5 billion.

Since the fifties the rate of growth of China's industrial output has averaged the remarkably high figure of 11

**Table 2.2**  National Expenditures 1979/80

|  | 1979 actual (billion yuan) | 1980 estimate (billion yuan) |
|---|---|---|
| Domestic capital | 44.38 | 37.35 |
| Expansion of existing enterprises | 7.20 | 6.98 |
| Bank funds | 5.20 | 3.72 |
| Agriculture (e.g., communes) | 9.01 | 7.74 |
| Education, culture, health, science | 13.21 | 14.83 |
| Military expenditures | 22.27 | 19.33 |
| Administration | 5.69 | 5.78 |

percent per year. The results are sometimes dramatic. For instance, Shanghai can now produce as much steel (some 5000 tons) in a few hours every morning as it took an entire year to produce in 1949. The municipality's total steel output is now (1978) over 5 million tons. The figures are somewhat artificial; 1949 was the year of Liberation and not much steel was produced; but growth has been rapid nonetheless.

However, it will not continue at such a rate. Gu Mu, vice premier and a skilled economist, said in October 1979 that the growth rate for 1979 was expected to drop to 8 percent and even lower for the remainder of the three-year period of restructuring and readjustment (1979–1981).

Wages are unlikely to drop in proportion. The fundamental principle of a fixed wage is part of the "iron rice bowl," the quasi-contractual agreement that each worker can keep his or her job without fear of replacement as well as, in most cases, being able to hand it to a son or daughter or even cousin. A worker's average annual income in 1979 ranged between 500 and 700 yuan for a factory worker and about 50–100 yuan for a rural peasant (the 80 percent majority). The official statistics for 1978 gave an average urban worker's wage as 614 yuan and an average peasant's wage as only 74 yuan (SWB/FEW/1058; XHNA, 5 October 1980). By 1980 the average annual wage of an urban worker had risen to 700 yuan, while the wages for those in the countryside had gone up to 80 yuan (SWB/FEW/1064). There is no income tax, except on the very high incomes that only foreigners can earn, and so these sums are the takehome pay.

The results of a government survey into the expenses of an average family in the city of Hangzhou, the capital of Chekiang province, are fairly illuminating of the cost of living (*Beijing Review*, 24 March 1980). The survey concentrated on the family of Feng Zhonglin and Shen Yuzhen, which consists of the father and mother, Shen's mother and two children. Incidentally, Shen Yuzhen was usually named first of the couple; in China, the woman is totally responsible for the family's finances.

Their combined monthly wages were 115.80 yuan, but they receive bonuses, and so forth, of about 38 yuan and a 17 yuan subsidy because their son is a student. The total, then, is 160.80 yuan a month. Each month Shen Yuzhen gives 10 yuan to her mother, leaving 30 yuan for each full member of the family. By far the biggest expense is food, which takes 60 yuan a month. Rent, water, and electricity cost a further 8.2 yuan. Feng's allowance (tobacco, wine, and so on) is 15 yuan, while the son is given 10 yuan and the daughter 2 yuan. Fifteen yuan is put aside for savings. After these basic expenditures the family has 45 yuan for "daily necessities and unexpected purchases."

A parallel survey analyzed the consumer goods being

bought by the people of Hangzhou. A sample 3238 families were interviewed about their purchases in the first eight months of 1980. The survey covered 12,628 people in all, just under four people per family. In those eight months they had bought 3653 bicycles (i.e., 1.13 per family), 1857 sewing machines (.57), 7665 wristwatches (2.37), 1687 radios (.52), 677 TV sets (.21), 221 record players (.07), 55 tape recorders (.02), 64 cameras (.02), and 1506 electric fans (.47).

For many years wages in China were inviolate. It was common to find a worker getting the same wage for 10 or 20 years. Such continuity, whether desirable or not, is unlikely to last much longer. The first reason is inflation, which is a newcomer to China but no less invidious for that. In 1979, the official rate of inflation, according to the State Statistical Bureau, was 5.8 percent. In November 1979 food prices rose in one jump by 33 percent and many workers negotiated wage increases to pay for their higher expenditures. Another reason is the highly significant move towards greater pay differentials and work schemes that provide bonuses, which Deng Xiaoping regards as crucial elements in the modernization program but which undoubtedly increase the money supply. At the same time the encouragement of trade has spurred consumer spending.

The arguments over prices and wages is only one aspect of the political battle now going on. The issue is the traditional one of setting policies and choosing methods that have and can be shown to have a direct and satisfactory link with the truth about the past as well as a practical suitability for today and tomorrow. The confrontation between Hua Guofeng and Deng Xiaoping was a battle about historical rectitude as much as a struggle for future power. Underlying all the fuss about the Gang of Four was the strong awareness in the country (except perhaps among the older cadres who owed their careers to the Cultural Revolution) that after the traumatic events of 1976–1977 it was no longer possible to pretend that China was on the verge of achieving the kind of national success that had been such a major aim since the revolution. The drunkenness and prostitution and gangs of unemployed youths (generally wearing a "uniform" of very shabby cotton clothes and very dark glasses) that emerged in Beijing and elsewhere towards the end of the 1970s were by no means the first to be seen in the People's Republic; but they gave an added edge to the urgency. The problem facing Deng and Hua was how to prosecute the Gang of Four so that the chosen leader could inspire the people to move forward into a new era of harmony. It was quintessentially a Chinese conundrum.

Hua's strength in 1976–1977 had been his avowed intimacy with Mao. By 1980 this friendship with the old man had become a liability. The reversals in Hua's fortunes were wonderfully illustrated by Hua's use of Mao's saying: "With you in charge, I am at rest." Nobody doubted that Mao had indeed given such a blessing. But when? And to Hua in charge of what? Hua has always maintained that Mao was referring to the governance of the PRC and that the phrase was a benediction of succession. He commissioned thousands of paintings and mosaics and rugs in which Mao is shown to be blessing the man from Hunan. But stories began to circulate that Mao had been referring not to the running of the country but to some rather smaller matter: a question of tactics, not statesmanship.

It was exactly these links with Mao that made Hua so vulnerable. The trial of the Gang of Four and the Lin Biao clique that opened in November 1980 was not only a trial of those in the dock but of all their colleagues and supporters, and that list of colleagues had Mao at the top and Hua not far below. As expected, Jiang Qing defended herself in part by saying that she was only following Mao's orders, sometimes with the tacit support of Hua. During the autumn and winter of 1980–1981 Hua saw his lineage of power had turned around and led nowhere.

At the very end of the year, while the trial was still in progress, there were several reports that Hua, who had resigned as prime minister in September, was soon to lose his chairmanship of the party. His replacement was to be Hu Yaobang, a protege of Deng.

# Chapter 3

## Broadcasting: Television and Radio

The broadcasting systems of most countries have evolved in a highly idiosyncratic fashion, and China is no exception. In many respects, the current system is even more complicated than might be expected because of the intricate relationship between state and party, and because of the party's sensitivity to all matters of mass communication.

The center of the broadcasting system is a massive building on Fuxingmen, the western extension of Beijing's main street, about a mile and a half from Tienanmen and the Forbidden City. This "broadcasting mansion," as it is often called, houses the Central Broadcasting Administration (CBA), the regulatory authority for all broadcasting policies and activities. The CBA reports directly to the Propaganda Committee of the CCP Central Committee, which has to ratify all its major policies. The mansion also houses China Central Television Station (CCTV), the national television service; the Central People's Broadcasting Station (CPBS), which provides the national radio service; and Radio International, the overseas service; not to mention the China Record Company, the Central Radio and TV Art Troupe, the Central Broadcasting Orchestra, the Broadcasting Institute, and the Broadcasting Research Institute.

Outside Beijing, all the municipalities, provinces, and autonomous republics operate TV and radio services, except Tibet, which has only radio. These regional stations receive guidance from the Central Broadcasting Administration, the Ministry of Culture, and the CCP at both national, regional, and local levels. There is a third level of cable or wired broadcasting, peculiarly Chinese, which delivers a mixture of retransmitted national or regional material and very local inserts. These "wire" services are distributed to over a hundred million loudspeakers in homes and public places. The only region of China without a proper TV service is Tibet. The Tibetan People's Broadcasting Station, which started in 1959 with two 3.5 kilowatt transmitters borrowed from the local posts and telecommunications bureau, does provide a radio service, distributed by two large central transmitters, relay stations in Qamdo, Shannan, Xigaze, Nagu, and Ngari, and 77 wired stations. But television has continued to be restricted to the trial service that started in Lhasa in May 1978 (WBI, 13 November 1980).

## TELEVISION

China began to experiment with television in 1956 through the efforts of the Central Broadcasting Science Research Factory and the Beijing Broadcasting Equipment Factory.

The USSR supplied most of the technical assistance and equipment. In 1958, as part of the Great Leap Forward, the Beijing government announced a four-year plan to establish a national network throughout the entire country. The plan was hugely ambitious and, like most of the Great Leap Forward, practically impossible.

Beijing Television started experimental broadcasts on 1 May 1958; regular schedules started on 2 September. The station had one studio with four image-orthicon cameras, one Outside Broadcast van, and one 1 kw transmitter (VHF, band 1, channel 2). The transmitter was fixed to the top of the CPBS building, about 220 feet above the ground. Its signals could be picked up throughout Beijing, although the capital could boast only a thousand sets at the time. By 1960, a dozen towns had stations, which, in the circumstances, was a remarkable achievement. All stations had to rely on films and tapes being "bicycled" from one to another. "Bicycling" is a universal term for sending TV material by any means, planes, cars, and so on, other than electronic transmission.

The break between China and the USSR (in June 1960) greatly hampered the development of all sectors of the economy. Broadcasting was no exception. The Russian engineers were sorely missed; spare parts were virtually unobtainable. Only in the late sixties did local manufacturing, and the development of technical institutes for training and research, manage to get the program of expansion moving again. Virtually all provinces had a TV station, and the stations in Beijing, Tianjin, Shanghai, and Canton were engineered for live broadcasting. In Beijing and Shanghai and other large cities, different TV programs began to be broadcast over two channels, one for news and entertainment, the other for education.

The four main stations, the country's largest, were

also connected by experimental microwave links. But the network was still young. The total output of all the transmitters was only 7.5 kw. During most of the Cultural Revolution (1966–1969) television stopped entirely. Many broadcasters were dismissed; equipment was not maintained; and policies were confused or absent. Recovery was very slow (in "The Universal Eye," Timothy Green recounts how in 1970 a visiting British broadcaster "counted up that 18 minutes out of a total 26 minutes of the main evening news bulletin one night were rolling captions of Mao's thoughts with background music of 'The East Is Red'."). The staple fare, it seems, consisted of the news, as described above, and the five Beijing operas approved by Jiang Qing.

Programs remained fairly straightforward for some years (mainly live relays and news), but many technical advances were made. In 1970 a research project was organized to study both the systems and the equipment for color television. Beijing Television, ever in the vanguard, began to experiment with color on 1 May 1973, and tests began in Shanghai, Guangzhou, Tianjin, and elsewhere. Indeed as the regional stations began to develop and assert themselves, the Beijing station began to have a dual role. It had to provide a national service to the regional stations while also providing the inhabitants of Beijing municipality with their own local service. On 1 May 1978, therefore (its twentieth birthday), a major structural reform was instigated. Beijing Television became the China Central Television Station (CCTV), responsible for both a national service and a regional service. And a brand-new organization, called Beijing Television, was inaugurated with the job of providing a separate Beijing service.

In 1980, television services were being supplied by China Central Television (CCTV), Beijing Television, and

36 other stations in the municipalities, the provinces, and the autonomous regions.

Programs are originated by all these stations. The CCTV originates two channels. The Beijing Municipal Station originates one channel; Shanghai, three channels; Tianjin, Guangzhou, and Chengtu, two channels; the remainder, one channel. In addition, all stations retransmit the CCTV national service. Therefore (with one exception), all audiences can receive the CCTV national service and their local service(s). The exception is Beijing, where it is possible to receive the CCTV national service, the CCTV's special Beijing service, and the local service provided separately by the Beijing Television station.

In Beijing, and everywhere else, the CCTV's first channel is broadcast as the primary service and any local service as the secondary service. However, audiences for the secondary service often match those for the first service when it deals with local events, dramas, and so forth. Another factor in audience preference is the dialect. The CTS uses putonghua, the common language, which is based on the Beijing dialect, while other services use the local dialect.

All stations use the USSR-sponsored 625-line, 50-hertz system which is now known as the "D" standard of television. It has a channel width of 8 MHz (relatively generous) and a vision bandwidth of 6 MHz (also generous). The sound signal is frequency modulated (FM).

China started to experiment with color television in 1973. It used both the PAL system, which had been developed by West Germany and is used by the UK and others, and the SECAM system developed by France and used by the USSR and in Eastern Europe. It chose PAL, and has developed its own version. The first station to switch to color was the CCTV. At the end of 1980, most

stations were colorized, although black-and-white programs are still being produced.

The bulk of studio equipment is China-made. Chinese
factories are now competent to produce cameras (both
film and video), most sound equipment, lighting equipment, and some tape recorders. There is an interesting
new range of color VTRs using one inch tape (No. SCL-1)
or half-inch tape (SD-292). The Shanghai Film Machinery
factory has also developed a magnetic film recording system; one model (LC35-6) can record six channels on 600
metres of 35mm stock. The film's footage and tension
are controlled by photoelectric cells. In the same league is
the Seagull series of flying-spot 35mm color telecine. The
telecine uses a cathode ray tube imported from the UK;
otherwise, all components are China-made. Sizes range
from 8.75mm to 35mm.

The main gaps in China-made equipment are in optics
and electronic editing. Most lenses are imported from
Japan; Canon lenses are very popular. As for VTR editing, the choice in China, as outside, is often Ampex. In
the small gauges of VTR and videocassette, Sony is equally prevalent.

Each station is responsible for originating its signal,
for transmitting the signal to the local transmitter, and for
transmission within its area. It is responsible for relay stations within its own area but not for relay stations outside
its boundaries. For instance, Tianjin is responsible for
transmitters within the municipality but is not responsible
for ensuring that nearby towns like Antze can receive the
signal. Nor is any central authority. Such nearby towns have
to raise their own funds, although the TV station would
probably provide technical assistance. The use of advertisements on TV will presumably provide some impetus to
stations to widen their coverage.

The Ministry of Telecommunications in Beijing is responsible for all trunk lines. Microwaves are used extensively.

Today, both the central and the regional stations are increasingly looking to other countries as a source not only of equipment but also of programs. In the past, China's exchanges with other countries have necessarily been erratic. The USSR, which supplied so much at the very beginning, ended its support abruptly in 1960. The few moves towards international agreements (such as an exchange agreement with Visnews in 1965) were sabotaged by the Cultural Revolution when all contacts with foreigners, especially in cultural matters, were banned. After 1969, foreign contacts were reestablished. China became a member of the Asian-Pacific Broadcasting Union (ABU) in December 1973 and has taken a leading role in ABU affairs.

In the last few years, many foreign broadcasters have visited China, and several Chinese delegations have visited Europe, Japan, and North America. The U.S. networks (led by ABC) and most European broadcasters have either signed or are preparing agreements of collaboration. There have been many documentaries made by foreign companies for showing on their domestic networks. The visits of Hua Guofeng and Deng Xiaoping to the USA and Europe were marked by numerous films by and about China.

The Chinese love to quantify, and statistics are regularly quoted to demonstrate the growth of the broadcasting services. The latest available figures are for 1979, when there were 99 central and local broadcasting (i.e., radio) stations, with 502 transmitting and relay stations, and 38 TV centers with 238 transmitting and relay stations with transmitters of more than 1 kilowatt (XHNA, October 1980, passim).

There is no satisfactory way of estimating the number

of TV and radio sets in China. Most estimates depend upon the figures for the number of sets that have been manufactured or imported, but these accumulated totals over the years take no account of the large number of sets that do not work or are not being used for some other reason. The low standard of many Chinese sets, and the paucity of good engineers, mean that a large number of sets are always out of order.

A Xinhua bulletin issued at the beginning of 1980 said that "one in every 280 Chinese people had a TV set as against one in 16,400 people ten years ago" (XHNA, 18 February 1980); says, 3.46 television sets. This figure is supported by several other sources. However, it must be remembered that a high proportion of sets do not work.

The rate of increase from sales and gifts is much harder to establish. The same note quoted the Ministry of Commerce that "1.42 million sets were sold last year, a nearly fourfold increase over 1978." However, a later note (XHNA, 30 April 1980) said sales of TV sets in 1979 went up by 200 percent over the 1978 figure. The source for the later note is the State Statistical Bureau, which might be regarded as more authoritative. As for gifts, usually from overseas Chinese, no figures exist.

The same State Statistical Bureau did give separate figures for the manufacture of TV sets. In 1979 output was put at 1,329,000, an increase of 157.1 percent over 1978, which gives a 1978 figure of .84 million. This increase is consistent with a 200 percent increase in sales but not with a 400 percent increase in sales. It is also not inconsistent with Hua Guofeng's remarks at the second session of the Fifth National People's Congress that 1979 output of black-and-white sets should be increased by "over 100 percent" from .5 million to 1.2 million.

It is confirmed by other sources. Towards the end of 1980 the Xinhua News Agency said that the "TV service reaches some five million TV sets, a figure soon to leap . . . China is expected to increase its TV sets by two to three million a year" (XHNA, 18 October 1980). Earlier the agency had said there were about 30 million television viewers (reported in *Beijing Review*, 21 July 1980) and that "the increasing number of TV sets and telecasts over an ever larger area have made television an important part of city life. In Beijing, one-third of the families have TV sets. In Shanghai, there is on average one set for every 4.2 households. In Guangdong, Fujian, Jiangsu, and other coastal provinces the number of households having TV sets is increasing. Taken as a whole, however, it is still a luxury to have a TV set in the countryside where 80 percent of the Chinese people live" (*Beijing Review*, ibid). The following week the Beijing Municipal Statistical Bureau announced that "the purchase of TV sets last year averaged 15 per 1000 families a month [a typically complex statistic] while the figure for April this year was 25.8 TV sets" (reported in *Beijing Review*, 28 July 1980). These figures relate only to the purchase of sets, of course. They do not begin to indicate how often the sets are used, nor do they help in estimating likely audiences for individual programs.

The manufacture of TV sets and TV equipment is seen as an important contribution to the modernization of the economy. There are regular announcements about increases in production and new deals. On 3 March 1980 *Beijing Review* reported that two new production lines for 12-inch black-and-white sets had gone into operation in Beijing, one with Chinese-made parts and the other with some imported machinery. The two lines will produce 240,000 sets a year. Another factory in Tianjin will produce 60,000 sets a year, ranging from 12 to 19 inches. The same report mentioned the opening of China's first color kinescope plant on the outskirts of Xianyang, Shaanxi, which will use Japanese machinery to produce 960,000 color kinescopes a year, with screens ranging from 14 inches to 22 inches.

The Xianyang factory is typical of the new trend towards joint ventures between a Chinese factory (often a well-established radio factory that wants to move into television) and a Western manufacturer. The country's first production line for color TV sets was imported from Japan in October 1980 (XHNA, 23 October 1980). In the same month the Chinese signed an agreement with the Corning Glass Works of the USA by which the Americans agreed to design and equip a 28,000 sq. ft. factory in Shanghai with the aim of producing about four million black-and-white tube envelopes by 1984.

Altogether, there are 40 "enterprises" producing TV sets, and in 1979 they produced 1.3 million sets, two and a half times as much as in 1978 (XHNA, 23 October 1980). Eight of these factories have made arrangements with Japanese companies to import color TV equipment (XHNA, passim). The Shanghai No. 1 Television Factory has bought an assembly line with an annual capacity of 200,000 color sets from Hitachi. A Beijing television factory and a Tianjin radio factory are buying a plant from Matsushita and JVC that will produce about 150,000 sets a year. The Suzhou TV Component Factory and the Beijing No. 3 Radio and TV Parts Factory will import production machinery with an annual capacity of 500,000 feedback transformers from JVC and Tokyo Sanyo Electric. Further deals have been signed with other Japanese components manufacturers and agents. A statement of the National Bureau of the Radio and Television Body (XHNA, 1 October 1980) said that "the government had invested 128 million yuan in the radio and television industry last year, twice the allocation made the previous year."

The price of TV sets varies from as little as 200 yuan for a Chinese-made 9-inch black-and-white set to about

2900 yuan for an imported Japanese 20-inch color set. Prices also differ considerably between towns. I saw the same Hitachi model for 2900 yuan in Beijing and for 2000 yuan in Chengtu, a thousand miles away in Sichuan province. In terms of average wages, even when families tend to pool their wages, these prices are very high.

## CCTV

The central television station (CCTV), China's main station, produces two services. Channel 2 is regarded as the primary service and is distributed to all stations by microwave and tape. Channel 8, the second channel, is distributed only within Beijing municipality. Both services are distributed by the same 7.5 kw transmitter (in comparison, the BBC and IBA main London transmitter, Crystal Palace, has 1000 kw of effective radiated power).

Channel 2 is normally on the air for eight hours a day. I was given the following format schedule. Obviously, each day is different; and a complete week's programs are given below.

| | |
|---|---|
| 8.30–<br>12 noon | The TV university: programs include science and technology, mathematics, English and other foreign languages, chemistry, computers |
| 5.30 | Educational programs for "middle school" children |
| 7.00 | National news |
| 7.15 | International news |
| 7.45 | Science and technology; also sports |
| 8.00 | Entertainment: Films, plays, etc. |

Channel 8, the second channel, which covers Beijing

only, has a more complicated schedule. It is arranged more by day of the week rather than by hour of the day. For instance, Monday, Wednesday, and Friday are devoted to educational programs, while Tuesday, Thursday, and Saturday concentrate on art and literature (both as education and as entertainment). On Sundays the station provides drama serials and more education. Total broadcasting is about 30 hours a week.

A list of the schedules for one specific week (24–30 September 1979) will show how these slots and strands take shape as actual programs.

*Monday 24 September*

*Channel 2*

5.30 P.M.  Basics of Semiconductor Circuits (No. 139)

6.20  English lesson (No. 3, 15-5)

7.00  News

7.20  Sports lovers: How to play bridge

7.40  The celebrations of the Thirtieth Anniversary of the Founding of Our People's Republic: A theater program relayed from Hebei province: "The Death Rays on Shanhu Island," performed by the Chengtu Regional Dance Group

*Channel 8*

7.00 P.M.  Algol programming (No. 20)

7.55  Basics of semiconductor circuits (No. 139)

8.50  English lesson (No. 3, 15-5)

9.20  News

*Tuesday 25 September*

*Channel 2*

5.30 P.M.  Algol programming (No. 21)

6.20    English lesson (No. 3, 15-5)

7.00    News

7.20    International knowledge

7.30    The celebrations of the Thirtieth Anniversary of the Founding of Our People's Republic: An opera program from Hunan province: "The Heroine from the Central Plains," performed by the Xiantan Opera Troupe

*Channel 8*

9.00 A.M.  Education (repeat of Monday's broadcast)

7.00 P.M.  Help yourself: Magazine program

7.20    Comedy: Birth control is good (a dialogue); chess

7.40    Film: "The Town of Dinglong"

9.20    News

*Wednesday 26 September*

*Channel 2*

5.30 P.M.  Basics of semiconductor circuits (No. 140)

6.20    English lesson (No. 3, 15-6)

7.00    News

7.20    Science and technology: Microwaves
Live broadcast of the finals of the Women's Volleyball Championship at the national games

| 10.00 | Science and technology: High-speed calculating; a brief introduction to six-digit division |

*Channel 8*

| 7.00 P.M. | Algol programming (No. 21) |
| 7.55 | Basics of semiconductor circuits (No. 140) |
| 8.50 | English lesson (No. 3, 15-6) |
| 9.20 | News |
| 9.35 | International knowledge |

*Thursday 27 September*

*Channel 2*

| 5.30 | Algol programming (No. 22) |
| 6.20 | English lesson (No. 3, 15-6) |
| 7.00 | News |
| 7.25 | Live coverage of the finals of the Men's and Women's Volleyball Championship at the national games (during the interval: International knowledge, and papercuts by Wang Zigan) |

*Channel 8*

| 9.00 A.M. | Education (repeat of Wednesday's programs) |
| 7.00 P.M. | Comic dialogue: Sons-in-law on trial |
| 7.20 | Film: "Morning Songs from the Prairie" |
| 9.20 | News |

*Friday 28 September*

*Channel 2*

| 3.23 P.M. | Live coverage of the State Council's |

prize-giving ceremony for national model workers in nationally advanced works in the front lines of industry, education, and capital construction

5.30    Basics of semiconductor circuits (No. 141)

6.20    English lesson (No. 3, 15-7)

7.00    News

7.20    Meeting of the Conference of Outstanding Workers

7.30    Comment by a TV journalist: Progressive development, light industries

7.55    Advice for living: Meat dishes

8.05    Animal world: The sand-fly

8.20    Film: "Liu Bao's Story"

*Channel 8*

7.00 P.M.    Algol programming (No. 22)

7.55    Basics of semiconductor circuits (No. 141)

8.50    English lesson (No. 3, 15-7)

9.20    News

9.35    World knowledge

*Saturday 29 September*

*Channel 2*

5.30 P.M.    Algol programming (No. 23)

6.20    English lesson (No. 3, 15-7)

7.00    News

7.15    Extracts from the performance by the pianist Huang Shunjing

| | |
|---|---|
| 8.15 | Meeting of the Conference of Outstanding Workers |
| 8.25 | World knowledge |
| 8.35 | Documentary: "The Rescue of the Titanic" |
| 8.50 | Help yourself: Magazine program |
| 9.00 | Culture: Guo Song, the folk singer |
| 9.40 | Documentary: "New Flowerings of Arts and Crafts in Chaozhou" |
| 10.00 | Film: "Spring Dreams of the Old Garden" (from Hong Kong) |

*Channel 8*

| | |
|---|---|
| 9.00 A.M. | Education (repeats of Friday's programs) |
| 7.00 P.M. | Folk art |
| 8.00 | Film: "The History of the Red Flag" |
| 9.20 | News |

*Sunday 30 September*

*Channel 2*

A collection of programs from Beijing and elsewhere to celebrate the thirtieth Anniversary of the Founding of Our People's Republic.

| | |
|---|---|
| 8.30 A.M. | From Shandong province:<br>A children's program, including a recital of poetry and fables<br>Film: "Who Is Best?"<br>Documentary: "The Temple of Yue Fei"<br>Opera: "Tales from the Top of the Wall, performed by the Bangzi Opera Troupe |
| 11.00 | From Guangdon province: |

The face of the Ling Mountain: Flower City and Green Sea
Music: Solo songs by Deng Yun
A children's film: "Two Little Brothers"
Opera: "Choose a Son-in-Law," with Wen Tuefei and the Guang Opera Troupe
Music and dance: Women singers
Dance: "Red Flowers on the Battlefield"

1.30 P.M.  From Shanghai:
News
Documentary: "Red Flowers on the Foothills of the Heaven Mountain," a documentary on the educated youth of Shanghai
"Shanghai Yesterday and Today": A hundred years of change in the concessions

2.00  From the central television station: "A Thousand Postures and a Hundred Poses Compete," an introduction to make-up by the Peking Opera

2.20  Children's program: A report on the visit of the Shanghai Children's Art Troupe to Yugoslavia

3.25  Live coverage of the banquet of the closing ceremony of the national games

5.25  Song and dance, performed by the Uigur Song and Dance Troupe from Xinjiang Autonomous Region

7.00  News

7.20  Live coverage of the Banquet of the State Council to celebrate the founding of the state

| 7.50 | Meeting of the Conference of Outstanding Workers |
|------|---------------------------------------------------|
| 8.00 | Around the world: Industry in Kuwait |
| 8.15 | Around China: The River Min flows on |
| 8.45 | Theater: "Future Summons," performed by the Central Experimental Theater Academy |

*Channel 8*

| 7.00 P.M. | Around China: The happy Dai people |
|-----------|-------------------------------------|
| 7.15 | Film: "Investigation of a Wife," from Hong Kong |
| 9.10 | News |
| 9.25 | World knowledge |

The CCTV has six policy departments and about ten program departments. The policy departments are the central editorial board (planning and public information, coordination, the general office and the secretariat); finance; general management; personnel; foreign affairs; and administration. The program departments are arranged in functional groups: news, feature one and feature two; videotape, film and technical matters, literature and art, international affairs, military affairs, and so on.

The current director of the CCTV is Li Lienching. Li is also deputy director of the Central Broadcasting Administration. The deputy director of the CCTV is Ren Yolin. (In China, the director of an organization is very often the deputy director of another, senior, organization; in practice, therefore, many organizations are actually run by deputy or vice directors.) Altogether, the CCTV has about 800 workers.

The CCTV has three studios, set at the back of the broadcasting mansion. The largest has 600 square meters;

the others have 180 square meters and 30 square meters. There are two control rooms, or "galleries," and two editing rooms. The station also makes extensive use of theaters in its own building and throughout Beijing. Most (70 percent) production is done with videotape; mostly 2-inch Ampex, but also some 1-inch (Type "C") and Sony's ¾-inch U-Matic System is used increasingly. About 20 percent of programs are made on film, and 10 percent are live. The station has four Outside Broadcast vans. It imported three (two from Japan in 1975 and one from the UK) and had one specially made in Shanghai in 1974. It also has a van with an ENG unit.

CCTV still uses the same transmitter tower as its predecessor did in 1967. The 180-meter tower has an effective power output of 50 kw on Channel 2 and 10 kw on Channel 8. All the transmitters have been made in Beijing or Shanghai.

The most popular programs, according to the CCTV, are films. Most films are made in China (see Chapter 6), but some are imported from Hong Kong, which may obviate the need to dub, and elsewhere. I was told the following foreign films have been shown by CCTV: "Death on the Nile" (UK), "The Million Pound Bank Note" (UK), "Oliver!" (Oliver Twist) (UK), "Carve Her Name With Pride" (UK), "A Respected Prostitute" (France), "Convoy" (USA), many Chaplin movies, and several from Yugoslavia.

It will surprise no one to be told that the Chinese, like every other society, are worried about the effects of TV on the cinema. As TV expands its coverage, and shows more movies, will people resent traveling to — and paying for — the cinema? So far (again, not unexpectedly), both the TV stations and the cinema tend to blame the other. I will discuss the problem, and current solution, in Chapter 6.

After films, the public seems to like news bulletins. The cause is very largely the satellite feeds that CCTV began to take from Visnews and UPITN in the first half of 1980 (as well as occasional, illegitimate pickups from Hong Kong). According to *Beijing Review*, 21 July 1980, "international news immediately became one of the most popular programs." It must have been fascinating for a country, so long isolated, to see newsfilm of the Iran hostages and the Iran-Iraq war (both specifically mentioned in the *Review's* report), indeed to see any pictures at all of the West.

China was the first country in the world to have a "television university." The Beijing Television College, serving Beijing only, started back in 1960, a full decade before the UK's Open University. The Beijing College and, later, the Shanghai College, were modest affairs, however, and the broadcast material was somewhat peripheral to the main educational effort. Both courses were stopped during the Cultural Revolution.

The current television university opened on 6 February 1979. It is regulated directly by the Central Broadcasting Administration under the auspices of the Ministry of Education. The relative roles of these two powerful bodies seems unclear. The confusion is perhaps not surprising because the planning and making of educational material on this scale, involving the professions of teaching and broadcasting, is an abstruse and intricate talent that has to be discovered anew by each TV university. The UK's Open University's principle of the "course team" is probably the most successful solution, and there have been several exchanges between the two universities. An additional problem faced by the Chinese is the division of responsibilities between the central authorities in Beijing and the provinces and municipalities. The Ministry of Education, the Central Broadcasting Administration, and the Central People's

Broadcasting Station are naturally dominant at a policy level, but the provincial educational ministries and broadcasting stations are taking an increasingly active part (notably the Shanghai TV Station). The main courses taught are mathematics, chemistry, English, and physics; each course lasts between one and one and a half years.

China has pressing needs for more and better education, at all levels; the people, on their part, have an insatiable desire to educate themselves. On 30 October 1979 some 600,000 people were reported in *Renmin Ribao* to have enrolled in one of the 29 television universities. To put that figure in perspective, it's worth saying that in the same year some 700,000 people had qualified for a place at a university or college, but only some 300,000 had been accepted, mainly because there were not enough places for everyone. Of that 600,000 total, therefore, over 400,000 were qualified to get to a regular, on-site campus. In another comparison, the UK's Open University enrolled 20,000 students.

One of the first entertainment programs to be made in China by a foreign company was a Bob Hope Special, "The Road to China," which NBC transmitted in September 1979. Future projects include several coproductions. A major French project, with a budget of £7 million, is "Man's Fate," based on André Malraux's story of the Shanghai Uprising of 1927. The director is Constantin Costa-Gavras. The Italian state broadcaster RAI is coproducing a version of "Marco Polo." It has been prefinanced by Procter and Gamble and Dentsu.

The flow is two-way. China has regularly bought foreign programs. Recently, its purchases have increased substantially. In late 1979 CCTV made China's first-ever purchase of a U.S. series, "The Man from Atlantis" (Taft-HB Productions). It bought the rights to show the series three times over the next four years; an unusually long-lived contract. In November it bought two series from the BBC, "Anna Karenina" and "David Copperfield," and a play, "Robinson Crusoe."

The Broadcasting Research Institute was set up in 1958, with Russian assistance. It is solely concerned with technical research. It monitors international developments and trends and makes recommendations to the CBA and individual stations. Its main function is to advise on the purchase of foreign equipment. None of the national organizations carries out research into audiences, either quantitative or qualitative. However, they do receive letters and telephone calls and have established local centers in the suburbs of Beijing where viewers can express their opinions. As in other areas, the organizations rely almost totally on the Communist Party and their own workers for evaluation and criticism. The Broadcasting Institute, like other institutes in China, is concerned with training, not with research. It trains employees in their professional tasks: technicians, announcers, directors, and journalists.

In the absence of a regular trade or professional association, the central organizations in Beijing often arrange meetings with their colleagues in other regions. In early 1979 for instance, CCTV organized a conference of all the directors of the regional stations. Some regions have also taken the initiative: Shanghai has instigated a series of quarterly meetings of the directors of six eastern provinces. The emergence of such horizontal groupings and alliances, following the example of the more aggressive filmmakers (see Chapter 4), may do much to speed the professional development of Chinese television, both in terms of its technical standards and in the quality of its programs.

Towards the end of 1980, in an important restructuring of CCTV, there emerged a new organization called the China Television Service, or CTVS. The CTVS im-

mediately became very active in several key areas: coproductions; buying and selling; satellite links; technical
liaison with foreign film crews; and advertisements on
CCTV's two channels. It was also responsible, it seemed,
for its own domestic film production units.

## The Beijing Television Station

The new Beijing Television Station started broadcasting
on 16 May 1978. It will be remembered from the previous
section that the "old" Beijing Television Station was restructured into CCTV in May 1978; there was a period of
two weeks before the new station was able to start regular
schedules.

Beijing Television is regulated by the municipal
branch of the CCP: to be exact, the Broadcasting Bureau
of the Propaganda Department of the Communist Party
Committee of the Municipality of Beijing. The Broadcasting Bureau regulates both Beijing Television and Beijing
Radio. (Beijing Radio is the local station and its name
should not be confused with the call sign of Radio Beijing, which is used by China's international services).

The old Beijing Television had two channels. The
new Beijing Television has only one, Channel 6, on VHF.
However, a second service, on Channel 13, may start in
the early eighties (on UHF). People in Beijing can therefore receive three TV channels at the moment (two from
the CCTV, one from Beijing Television), with prospects of
a fourth. The station uses one 10 kw VHF transmitter
whose coverage, I was told, varies between 10 and 20
kilometers. It is powerful enough to cover the city and
most of the suburbs. In addition, it covers 20–30 percent
of the municipality's territory and 70–80 percent of its
population.

The aim of Beijing Television is to have four hours of

instructional programs and two hours of general programs each day. However, this output is not achieved yet on a regular basis, as can be seen from the listed schedules for a week in September 1979.

*Channel 6*

*Monday 24 September*
7.00 P.M.   News in brief

7.05        Documentary: "Hunting in Winter"

7.20        Opera: "The Sunny Ravine"

*Wednesday 26 September*
7.00 P.M.   News in brief

7.05        Documentary: "To Build a Golden Bridge"; "For Generations of Friends"

8.00        Film: "The Hairdresser"

*Friday 28 September*
7.00 P.M.   News in brief

7.05        Selections from Chinese opera;
            Selections from new productions performed by the students of the Beijing Traditional Opera School, Yu Cangjian, Er Jingong

*Sunday 30 September*
7.00 P.M.   News in brief

7.05        Music: "Sing the Praises of the Daughter of the Party, Zhang Zhixin" (recorded by Shandong province TV Station)

7.30        An Introduction to Beijing Folk Opera: "Singing Heartily, New Voices Add to the Spring's Rays" (recorded by the Shanghai Television Station)

8.00    Opera: "The Magnificent Wedding Ceremony," performed by the Marine Administration Opera Troupe

The station has 60 workers, organized into an editorial department, with management teams and production
teams, and a technical department. There is one studio,
about 40 square meters, which is used for both film and
TV. It has four electronic cameras: one color camera, two
black-and-white cameras, and one minicam. All cameras
are Song Hua Giang brand, made in Shanghai; a few
lenses, however, are imported. The VTRs are Sony 200P
and 2860; they also use Sony's ¾-inch U-Matic and, I was
told, they are not above using ¾-inch tape for recording
and transmission.

Clearly, the station has very few resources. It is very
much overshadowed by CCTV. The relationship between
the two stations is not helped, of course, by the fact that
the CCTV is simply the former Beijing Television Station
writ large; undoubtedly it has kept the best facilities and
can attract the best workers. Nonetheless, the Beijing Television Station has some interesting plans for the future
which it is more than capable of fulfilling. Its current six-
year plan (1980–1985) has three priorities. The first is to
extend coverage to near 70 percent of the municipality by
setting up VHF relay stations in each of the 13 counties.
Second, it will produce many more educational programs
and expand the television university to some seven hours
a day. At present (XHNA, 19 May 1980), the Beijing
Television university has over 40,000 students, which is
three times the annual enrollment of the city's 49 regular
institutions of further education. Most of its university
programs, however, will be taken from the CCTV. Third,
it will expand the slot for general programs from two to
four hours daily, and run them regularly between 6 and

10 P.M. It will start a drama section. In October 1979 the station stopped prerecording its regular "News in Brief" program and went live, as an experiment. At the time of writing, the experiment is being judged a success.

The station decided to accept advertising on a paid basis, on 1 November 1979. Previously, it had carried only public service announcements about new products. The cost per second starts at 60 yuan for Chinese products and 180 yuan for foreign products. More details are given in Chapter 10.

## Shanghai Television Station

The Shanghai Television Station started broadcasting in 1958, when there were reputed to be 2000 sets in the area. It is regulated in the same manner as the Beijing Television Station, by the municipal CCP, through its Propaganda Department's Broadcasting Bureau. It has one main 10 kw transmitter and several relay stations. Together, they cover the entire municipality (3600 square miles). In addition, the towns of Suzhou and Wuxi in Tiangsu province to the north, and towns in the other neighboring provinces of Zheijiang and Anhui to the west and south, can receive the station's signals with the help of the municipality's transmitters and their own relay stations.

The station's workers estimate the number of TV sets in the municipality to be around 500,000. They base their estimate partly on the fact that the weekly program journal regularly prints 400,000 copies and always sells out; but these sales, of course, indicate the number of viewers, not the number of sets. However, there is no denying the fact that the newspaper is popular: many copies are pasted on walls, others are rented for two hours for half the cover price. The workers also estimate that there are about 100,000 sets in Suzhou and Wuxi, and a further 200,000 within the overall reception area, bringing the total number to 800,000.

Shanghai Television distributes two channels: its own Channel 5 and Channel 8, which is substantially a retransmission of CCTV's primary service. Channel 5 starts at 7 A.M. and continues to 9 or 10 P.M.; there is a 1½-hour break at lunchtime. Channel 8 broadcasts for two hours in the morning between 9 and 11 A.M. and again between 5 and 10 P.M. in the evening. The station is thus on the air for a total of 19½ hours. However, due to the practice in Shanghai of having several minutes break between each program, the actual total is nearer 18 hours a day. (This practice is not exclusive to Shanghai; but Shanghai seems to take it to the extreme.) Shanghai has always been noted for its flourishing, cosmopolitan arts: literature, theater, the cinema, and so on. The Shanghai Television Station naturally exploits this tradition and often relays local plays and operas as well as producing its own political satires on local events. The station started to accept paid advertisements in February 1979, on Channel 5 only, and generally sells about three minutes a day. The rates for Chinese organizations are "by negotiation"; foreign companies pay 2800 yuan per minute.

The station has a director and a deputy director and five departments: news, editorial, engineering, the general office, and administration. The general office is the central management office, with responsibilities for budgeting, overall strategy, and scheduling. There are a total of 300 workers. There are two studios, one of 600 square meters and one of 300 square meters. The station needs more space. I once saw two programs being recorded (or, at least, rehearsed) in the same studio. The floors of both studios are covered with the finest parquet flooring, which looks nice, but is noisy and uneven and difficult to keep clean. The workers are aware of the problem and have added "rubber flooring" to their long list of needed equipment.

The cameras are Chinese, with Canon zoom lens (P10 × 20B4, whose focal length is 20–200 mm) imported from Japan. The mix is typical; the Chinese are competent at the electronics but have not got the equivalent skills and equipment in optics. There is one Sony BVP/200P lightweight camera in regular use in the studio; it feeds into a U-Matic VTR. The station has two Ampex second-generation 2-inch VTRs with added Tektronics electronics, and two U-Matics. It also has a Sony videorecorder (1000PSOT, BVH 1000PS). All the tapes that I saw were Sony.

The station has long been wanting to transmit on the UHF band and it may well begin to do so in 1981. The BBC monitoring service picked up an announcement by the Shanghai People's Broadcasting Station, the radio service, that TV transmissions could start on Channel 20 in January 1981 (WBI, 13 November 1980). It would be China's first use of UHF for broadcasting.

## RADIO

The Chinese have always regarded radio as more important than television. The reasons are fairly obvious (and equally apparent to many other Third World countries). The technology is simpler and cheaper and, partly for those reasons, radio's coverage is far wider. Also, the medium lends itself to words, to information and discussion, whether for dogma and ideology, or for participation and access.

There are three levels of radio stations. The dominant station is the Central People's Broadcasting Station (CPBS), which was founded in 1949 and now transmits several national and regional programs. There are also 87 regional stations operated by provinces, municipalities, autonomous regions and cities, with a further ten stations of roughly similar administration, making a total of 97 regional stations. Most regional stations provide two channels (each duplicated on several different frequencies), although Shanghai has as many as five and Beijing has four. Shanghai's fifth channel started on 5 November 1979 with promises of many music programs; for extra quality, the channel is being broadcast on VHF/FM.

The third level consists of county stations and relay stations. Here, there are chronic difficulties of definition. The CPBS states there are 22 million relay stations. Clearly, these stations are simply relay stations in the usual technical sense of the word. They cannot edit a program's content. Yet many relay stations do exactly that: producing and editing programs to make them more suitable to the locality. On the basis of previous analyses and my own discussions I would estimate that there are probably 1500 to 2500 stations that, at the county level, operate to some extent the functions of production and editing.

In Beijing it is possible to receive as many as seven different programs: two programs from the CPBS, four from the municipal station, and one from a local station. In Shanghai, with five municipal channels, it is possible to receive as many as eight. But these figures are exceptional. Most Chinese would count themselves fortunate to get one "central" channel and one local channel; and many are not so lucky.

The ability to receive a program, of course, does not equate with the ability to understand it. China has many dialects of varying degrees of intelligibility. The Beijing dialect (putonghua) is spoken by no more than 70 percent of the population. In some country areas the CPBS's programs, spoken in the best Beijing (mandarin) dialect, as BBC programs were long spoken in "Oxford" English, were incomprehensible to most of the people. In Wenshou, in southern Zhejiang, the station once complained that putonghua could only be understood by a minimal 5 percent of the population; and even the Wenzhou dialect could only be understood by people within about 35 miles of the town. Many stations have found it impossible to communicate with a majority of their target population simply because the population, in terms of their dialects, is unavoidably composed of a series of exclusive minorities.

A major feature of the radio services is their distribution by wire to public loudspeakers. These loudspeakers are not quite omnipresent but during the mid-morning break or on public holidays it is difficult to escape their sound. They are mainly located in places of work (factories, the fields, communes) but are also pervasive in the streets, in public places, in parks, and so on. It is through these loudspeakers, which are counted in tens of millions, that the real nature of Chinese radio is most readily apparent.

## History

The first, celebrated, radio station of the Chinese Communist Party started transmitting on 5 September 1945. It was the Yanan Xinhua Broadcasting Station, which soon became better known as the Northern Shaanxi Xinhua Broadcasting Station. In March 1949 that station's workers took their equipment to Beijing where they set up the organization that on 1 October was named the Central People's Broadcasting Station.

The importance of radio to the Communist Party ensured that it expanded rapidly, both at the national level, and in the distribution of services to communes, brigades, and teams. In the fifties, the priority was on the former. In 1950 there were reckoned to be some 2000 loudspeakers in the entire country; by 1960 there were 4.5 million (CCP figures). In the following years, the priority seems to have been to broaden the appeal of the programs, as well as to ensure the widest possible distribution.

Today, trunk transmission is by over-the-air radio links; the signals are then either rebroadcast over the air or retransmitted by wire. The Central People's Broadcasting Station estimates that there are about 50 million radio sets capable of receiving over-the-air broadcasts and about 120 million loudspeakers in the wired network. Both figures fit well with the majority of independent estimates.

If accurate, the figures imply that some 5 percent of households have a private radio set and that some 90 percent of households have a loudspeaker in or near their place of work. The CPBS has the widest coverage of all stations, yet it reaches only 25–30 percent of households. The myriad local stations are the sources of radio for most of the population. But the difference is not as great as it might appear. Many of the local country stations simply "rip and read" from the CPBS or the Xinhua News Agency.

At the beginning of 1980, "one in 11 Chinese possesses a radio set," according to a Xinhua bulletin of 18 February 1980; say, a total of 88,180,000. These sets could be either portable, transistorized sets, or mains sets. Some sets would be very old.

As a footnote, it is interesting to quote from *Chung Yang Jih Pao*, a Taiwan newspaper, which said on 16 August 1979 that a pirate radio station, the Voice of the People, in Hsiangchiang, Hunan, was transmitting regular broadcasts that were "hostile to the national and local authorities." Such dissident broadcasts are fairly common in communist countries (most notably Yugoslavia) but I believe this station is the first to be reported in China. Another similar station, First August Radio, which is hostile to Deng Xiaoping, was first heard in October 1979.

## The Central People's Broadcasting Station

The Central People's Broadcasting Station (CPBS) is the largest and probably the dominant organization within the central sector. Its preeminence stems from its origins, from the tacit acceptance of radio as the most important broadcast medium, and from the sheer size of the organization. Like CCTV, the CPBS reports direct to the State Council. But, even more so than CCTV, it is in practice regulated by the Communist Party at the highest level. The formal regulatory body is the Propaganda Committee, which reports directly to the Central Committee. But CPBS policies and programs are very much part of the daily routine of the Communist Party; they are embedded in the party's essential consciousness; they are one of the purest expressions of party policy and politicking. Its policies and programs are therefore matters which the party leadership would naturally keep under its own tight control.

The CPBS currently broadcasts over five channels. Two channels in putonghua are broadcast throughout the mainland for a total of 40 hours a day. A third, in putonghua and the Fujian and Kejia dialects, is transmitted to Taiwan, for about 20 hours a day. The fourth channel is aimed at national minorities and uses the Kazak, Korean, Mongolian, Tibetan, and Uygar languages; it broadcasts for about 10 hours a day. The fifth channel serves the overseas Chinese (in Hong Kong, etc.) and broadcasts both putonghua and the Guangzhou, southern Fujian, and Kejia dialects. It broadcasts for about 20 hours a day. Each day, therefore, the CPBS broadcasts a grand total of some 90 hours of programs. A third national channel, of literature and the arts, may start in 1980–1981.

The organization of the CPBS is rather complicated, both because of its size and because of the sensitivity of its task. The highest body is the General Editorial Office, which is actually part of the Central Broadcasting Administration. This office administers eight major departments: news (sometimes called the permanent news department); special features; a department for workers, peasants, and soldiers; a department for literature and the arts; a department for nationalities (in China, that means the national minorities); a department for youth and children; a presentation department (continuity, announcers); a department for overseas Chinese, and a department for broadcasts to Taiwan. Each of these administrative departments contains its own departments for production, engineering, and so forth. In all, the CPBS has 1000 workers (in addition to a considerable number of the 700 workers employed by the Central Broadcasting Administration).

The content of programs on the first two channels can be broken down into news (15 percent); features (25 percent); and literature, art, and music (55 percent). The bulk of the news comes from the Xinhua News Agency, which supplies the CPBS with upwards of 50,000 words a day of national and international news and news summaries. The CPBS formats this input into 29 bulletins a day, many of which run for 30 minutes. A typical long bulletin would have 10 minutes of "soft" news, 5 minutes of news in brief, and 15 minutes of background information.

The features are broadly educational. I was given these subjects as examples: the life of the People's Liberation Army; the study of Marxism-Leninism; the study of science and technology; hygiene; reading and appreciation; and a popular series called "Across the Motherland," which presents distant or unusual events, achievements, and traditions. The largest component of the literature and art programs is music; it constitutes 30 percent of the category, 10 percent of total air time. Other popular programs are drama and opera.

In the first flush of excitement after the arrest of the

Gang of Four, from late 1976 to March 1979, the CPBS, like most other cultural organizations, swung enthusiastically into producing more programs on the arts. The emphasis is still evident; 55 percent of the total is a remarkably high percentage. Now, following the second session at the Fifth National People's Congress, the CPBS is planning to readjust the proportions of program output in accordance with the needs of the four modernizations; in practice that means more educational programs. A major plank in the new policy is the idea for a radio university to match the highly successful television university.

## BEIJING RADIO

Beijing Radio is the municipality's own radio station (not to be confused with Radio Beijing, which is the common term, derived from its call sign, for Radio International). Beijing Radio is regulated like Beijing Television; that is, by the CCP's local Broadcasting Bureau. It started in 1949, by taking over the Nationalists' station.

It has four channels, known as the news channel (about one third of whose programs are taken direct from the CPBS); the music channel; "features"; and "languages." The latter provides lessons in English, French, and Japanese. Each channel is on the air for about 15–16 hours a day. The channels are distributed by means of four 7.5 kw transmitters to about 60 percent of the municipality's area and to about 80 percent of its population. The station is run by a general office and is divided into an editorial department, with about 140 workers, and an engineering department, with about 110 workers. It has 11 studios, of which 8 are in general use.

Over the next few years the station sees as its main priority the replacement of its old, if not ancient, equipment. Some of the microphones and audio recorders date from pre-Liberation times. Other aims are a separate channel for education, and a channel to provide 24-hour entertainment and culture. The news department also wants to recommence the practice, common before the Cultural Revolution, of doing live news bulletins. It hopes that its regular news program, "News in Brief," which goes out six times a day, at 9 A.M., 10 A.M., 12 noon, 4 P.M., 8.30 P.M., and 9 P.M., will be able to go live in 1981. Other programs may have to wait for several years.

## RADIO INTERNATIONAL

Radio International, whose call sign is the more familiar Radio Beijing, is China's sole overseas service. It started broadcasts in 1950, with seven languages. Today, it provides services in 39 different languages as well as putonghua and four Chinese dialects. Each day it transmits a total of 121 hours of programing. The station is generally regarded as the world's third largest international broadcaster after Radio Moscow and the U.S. stations. See table 3.1.

A vital factor in the strength of an international broadcasting service is the location and power of the transmitters. In this respect the U.S. services and the BBC's External Services have always been especially fortunate (although the BBC is being forced to close several transmitters for reasons of national economy, a move which puzzles the Chinese enormously). China has very few places where she can establish the necessary transmitters. The major problem is the break with Albania, which has meant that Europe's reception of Radio Beijing is very patchy. Broadcasts to Europe are now transmitted by relay stations in Xinjian and Tibet.

There is some talk by station staff of a communications satellite that will solve virtually all transmission problems. It is true that a communications satellite, probably in a

**Table 3.1** Radio Beijing Schedule for English-Language Transmissions as from 30 October 1979

| GMT | Local Standard Time | Meter bands | kHz |
|---|---|---|---|
| | | **North America (East Coast)** | |
| 00.00–01.00 | 19.00–20.00 (E.S.T.) | 19, 16 | 15115, 15520, 17680 |
| 01.00–02.00 | 20.00–21.00 (E.S.T.) | 19, 16 | 15115, 15520, 17680 |
| 02.00–03.00 | 21.00–22.00 (E.S.T.) | 19, 16 | 15115, 17680, 17855 |
| 12.00–13.00 | 07.00–08.00 (E.S.T.) | 25 | 11685 |
| | | **North America (West Coast)** | |
| 03.00–04.00 | 19.00–20.00 (P.S.T.) | 25, 24, 19, 16 | 11685, 12055, 15300, 17680 |
| 04.00–05.00 | 20.00–21.00 (P.S.T.) | 25, 24, 19, 16 | 11685, 12055, 15300, 17680 |
| | | **Australia and New Zealand** | |
| 08.30–09.30 | 18.30–19.30 (Aust. E.S.T.)<br>20.30–21.30 (N.Z.S.T.) | 31, 25, 19, 17 | 9460, 11600, 11725, 15125, 17635 |
| 09.30–10.30 | 19.30–20.30 (Aust. E.S.T.)<br>21.30–22.30 (N.Z.S.T.) | 31, 25, 19, 17 | 9460, 11600, 11725, 15125, 17635 |
| | | **East and South Africa** | |
| 16.00–17.00 | 18.00–19.00 (Cape Town, Salisbury)<br>19.00–20.00 (Dar-Es-Salaam) | 30, 19 | 9860, 15315 |
| 17.00–18.00 | 19.00–20.00 (Cape Town, Salisbury)<br>20.00–21.00 (Dar-Es-Salaam) | 30, 19 | 9860, 15315 |

**Table 3.1** Radio Beijing Schedule for English-Language Transmissions as from 30 October 1979 (*continued*)

| GMT | Local Standard Time | Meter Bands | kHz |
|---|---|---|---|
| | | Southeast Asia | |
| 13.00–14.00 | 20.00–21.00 (Western Indonesia, Bangkok) | 32, 25, 19, 16 | 9290, 11650, 15270, 17700 |
| | 20.30–21.30 (Singapore) | | |
| | 21.00–22.00 (Ho Chi Minh City, Manila) | | |
| | 19.30–20.30 (Rangoon) | | |
| | | South Asia | |
| 14.00–15.00 | 19.30–20.30 (Delhi, Colombo) | 30, 25, 19 | 9860, 11650, 15315 |
| | 19.00–20.00 (Rawalpindi) | | |
| | 20.00–21.00 (Dacca) | | |
| | 19.40–20.40 (Kathmandu) | | |
| 15.00–16.00 | 20.30–21.30 (Delhi, Colombo) | 30, 25, 19 | 9860, 11650, 15315 |
| | 20.00–21.00 (Rawalpindi) | | |
| | 21.00–22.00 (Dacca) | | |
| | 20.40–21.40 (Kathmandu) | | |
| 18.00–19.00 | 23.30–00.30 (Delhi) | 247 | 1206 |

**Table 3.1** Radio Beijing Schedule for English-Language Transmissions as from 30 October 1979 *(continued)*

| GMT | Local Standard Time | Meter Bands | kHz |
|---|---|---|---|
| | | West and North Africa | |
| 19.30–20.30 | 18.45–19.45 (Monrovia) | 30, 25, 19 | 9880, 11695, 15100 |
| | 19.30–20.30 (Accra, Freetown) | | |
| | 20.30–21.30 (Lagos) | | |
| | 21.30–22.30 (Cairo) | | |
| 20.30–21.30 | 19.45–20.45 (Monrovia) | 30, 25, 19 | 9880, 11695, 15100 |
| | 20.30–21.30 (Accra, Freetown) | | |
| | 21.30–22.30 (Lagos) | | |
| | 22.30–23.30 (Cairo) | | |
| | | Europe | |
| 20.30–21.30 | 21.30–22.30 (London, Stockholm, Paris) | 43, 40, 26 | 6860, 7470, 11500 |
| 21.30–22.30 | 22.30–23.30 (London, Stockholm, Paris) | 43, 40, 26 | 6860, 7470, 11500 |
| | | Southeast Asia | |
| 12.00–13.00 | 19.00–20.00 (Western Indonesia, Bangkok) | 32, 25, 19, 16 | 9290, 11650, 15270, 17700 |
| | 19.30–20.30 (Singapore) | | |
| | 20.00–21.00 (Ho Chi Minh City, Manila) | | |
| | 18.30–19.30 (Rangoon) | | |

geostationary orbit, and broadcasting at 1 GHz, is being considered by some countries for sound broadcasting. But such a system requires an elaborate antenna that, in practice, will have to be fixed in one spot; it could not supply the casual listener.

The programs consist mostly of the same material, irrespective of destination. The main content categories are news (25 percent), comment (15 percent), information on China (30–50 percent) and music (about 20 percent). The information on China is usually about culture or art, geography, and so forth; politics is mentioned very seldom. Everything is prerecorded.

The station reports to the Central Broadcasting Bureau but is also closely linked to the Central People's Broadcasting Station; it is, to some extent, the overseas arm of the CPBS. It is, of course, also dependent on the Propaganda Committee of the party, and has the reputation of being the most tightly controlled of the various broadcasting organizations. The 1000 workers are divided into language groups, as in the U.S. services and the BBC's External Services. There are the unusually large number of 36 vice presidents, and there is some concern that the organization is rather fragmented. In November 1979, some sections were amalgamated. The most important group is the Japanese section, which has five experts (and a total of about 100 workers). The English section has two experts (and 70 workers); and the French section has one expert (and 40 workers). The Chinese have always supported the development of Esperanto which they hope might provide a common ground for people who use roman alphabets and people who use ideographs, hiragana characters, and so on. The Esperanto section has two experts.

All the sections depend greatly on the news and features that are prepared by the Xinhua News Agency. The XHNA material arrives partly translated; nevertheless, the most substantial single function of each language group is the translation of this and other material. Apart from the experts, who are generally foreigners, and who speak the language concerned as their first language, the workers in each section share the duties of translation, typing, presentation, and maintenance. There is little evidence of any hierarchy within each group; at the same time, there is little evidence of functional responsibility. The reason is probably the rigid dependence on the Communist Party's guidelines, the material supplied by the XHNA, and the overall control exercised by the General Editorial Office.

The Cultural Revolution and the actions of the Gang of Four deeply influenced Radio International. The staff spoke to me of "sabotage" and "confusion." Certainly, for many years, the programs were often dull and uninformative. The station's staff said many overseas listeners complained that they could not understand what the station was saying. Today, the station is making better use of the medium. But the workers still complain of the backward equipment and the lack of powerful transmitters. They are proud that the station has only Chinese-made equipment but acknowledge that the station's aims would be well served by importing foreign equipment if they had sufficient foreign currency. It is a common dilemma.

# Chapter 4

## Film

In a sustained burst of creativity, China's film studios are now producing more films on a wider range of topics than for many years. The classic operas, novels, and plays will continue to provide sources of enlightenment and enjoyment in their peculiarly Chinese manner, but film more neatly symbolizes the modern age, and the new freedom given to the studios allows film to play a leading role in the emerging consciousness of modernization. The new films can be very specific about recent political events. The "Laughter of a Distressed Man," for instance, was based explicitly on the true story of a Shanghai journalist who was abused by the Gang of Four. Many of its characters are recognizable from real life. Moreover, these films can communicate with the ordinary, even illiterate, Chinese to a degree that the classic literature can never do. The crowds outside a cinema remain long after the cinema has closed. It is a meeting place for people who want to meet and talk.

The history of film in China is a mark of the country's varying attitudes to foreign developments. At the very end of the last century the Beijing government was making films only a year after the Lumiere brothers, on the other side of the world, had given their first demonstration. Yet in the middle of this century the Chinese virtually stopped all imports of foreign films.

China acquired its first film equipment in 1896. Within a few years, by 1903, Pathé newsreels were being shown regularly in Shanghai. In 1913 the Asian Motion Picture Company was set up. During the next two decades Chinese films were mostly derivative of U.S. films (as were the films of Japan, Hong Kong, and many other countries). Among the more notable were "The Lost Kids," "Street Angels" and "The Spring River Flows East," which still gets large audiences. The emerging communists soon began to make their own revolutionary films (e.g., "Song of the Fisherman," "Cross Roads"), although their primitive facilities meant that their films were more enjoyed for the novelty of the medium than for any particular content. The communist cause was assisted in 1937 when Joris Ivens, a Dutch filmmaker, gave the party its first 16 mm camera, an event which has come to assume major symbolic importance.

After Liberation, in 1950–1951, the eight film studios which were operating in Shanghai were combined into today's Shanghai Film Studios; similar amalgamation occurred in Beijing. Other film studios were set up in Changchun, Xi'an, and other cities. The August First Film Studios were set up in Beijing for the army. From 1949 to 1957 the industry produced a total of 170 films, an average of about 20 a year. During the Great Leap Forward of the next three years, it is often claimed that production increased by 500 percent or more, to a 1958 total of 103, but these claims may be for quotas rather than for completed films. The Shanghai Film Studios have told me that their best-ever production was in 1956 when they produced 18 features.

There is no doubting, however, the dire effects of the Cultural Revolution. The leader of the Gang of Four, Jiang Qing, had been an actress at the Shanghai Film Studios; she was remembered by most of the staff as an actress with not much skill. Jiang Qing wreaked a special kind of vengeance on her old colleagues.

She imprisoned 15 directors and actors. She restricted some two-thirds of the remainder to "house arrest" in a building they called the "cow-shed." And she sent some to schools for communist cadres, to be reeducated. Zhao Dan, the country's most famous actor, who starred in "Street Angel" (1937), "Crows and Sparrows" (1949), and "Li Shizhen, The Great Pharmacologist" (1956), was imprisoned for five years. When released, according to the magazine *Chinese Literature*, he was unable to "speak, move, or act like a human being." Other actors did not survive their imprisonment. She also blacked all the features that the studios had made since 1949. The films remained blacked for seven years until 1973. Some films were produced during the Cultural Revolution, but I have been told — half seriously — that they were so dull nobody watched them.

Since the mid-seventies, and especially since the rise of the new leadership, the cinema has regained its former status and has become, more than ever, a touchstone of China's cultural mood. Production has continued to increase. In 1977, 28 feature films were produced; in 1978, 40; and in 1979, a total of 65 (the quota for 1979 was 54). Altogether, 139 new full-length films of different types were distributed in 1979, according to the State Statistical Bureau (XHNA, May, passim). In 1979 about 70 films were imported for exhibition and study. The major suppliers were Japan, the UK, and the USA. Of other communist countries, Yugoslavia was the most popular. From the UK, the China Film Corporation imported "The Slipper and the Rose," "The Voyage of the Damned," "Jane Eyre," and "Death on the Nile," which EMI claim is the most popular foreign film in China. The U.S. films included "Nightmare in Badham County," "Cabaret," "Rebecca," "Intermezzo," and "Convoy." "The Sound of Music" was also bought, because it was "antifascist." The average price for a foreign movie is £5000.

## REGULATION

The main regulatory body for the film industry is the Ministry of Culture's Film Bureau. A separate body, the China Film Corporation, which describes itself as a branch of the Film Bureau, is responsible for day-to-day matters. The Film Bureau is responsible for policy and planning. It allocates quotas to each studio and arranges matters of pricing, resources, and distribution. The relationship between bureaucrats and filmmakers is seldom a happy one; China is no exception. In the last few years there have been several ructions. Some filmmakers call the ministry the "mother-in-law."

Gradually, the filmmakers seem to be winning greater freedom. There are two reasons for the change. The first is that the new spirit of independence and decentralization allows individuals and groups to work without continual supervision. Secondly, the success of the new wave of films at the box office publicly confirms the filmmakers' own judgments about what the masses really want. Of course, the CCP monitors and checks the work in prog-ress. An example of the changes is that the ministry has abdicated its rights to see scripts before filming started. In the past, each script had to be submitted to Beijing, which took time and could generate some rambling discussions. Today, the studio can move directly to production. The change followed a meeting of all studio directors in Febru-ary 1979 to discuss the relationship between the Film Bureau and the studios. It was the first of a regular series of meetings held to emphasize the filmmakers' profession-al standing. They were saying that they were expert, not red, and that experts should be allowed to exercise their expertise.

The China Film Corporation (CFC) is the industry's main specialist and executive organization. It was formerly (until 1979) called the China Film Distribution and Ex-hibition Corporation. Its main functions are to monitor and advise the industry. It buys all the films produced by Chinese studios and organizes their distribution and ex-hibition. It also exports and imports. The CFC is con-cerned with ensuring that the current race to produce more films (after the Gang of Four's cutback) is paralleled by a desire to produce better films. As the general direc-tor said to me, "We want to encourage Mao's teaching, 'Let 100 flowers bloom,' but we want the flowers to be well tended."

As an aid to this improvement a Chinese Society of World Cinema, the country's first organization for film studies, has been formed in Beijing. At the inaugural meeting on 25 March 1980, over 200 professional and amateur enthusiasts heard Meng Guangjun, secretary general of the Chinese Film Association, express the new society's hope that a study of foreign films would "help develop China's own films."

## PRODUCTION

There are 15 film studios in China making films for general distribution. Many more, in factories, schools, and communes make films for their own use. In China as in the West the production of feature films for theatrical release is only a small proportion of the total. In Beijing there are:

> The Beijing Film Studios
>
> The August First Film Studios, operated by the People's Liberation Army and named to celebrate the founding of the PLA on 1 August 1927
>
> The Central News and Documentary Film Studios
>
> The Science and Technology Film Studios
>
> The Education Film Studios
>
> The Agricultural Film Studios

Shanghai, which is the birthplace of Chinese filmmaking, has:

> The Shanghai Film Studios
>
> The Shanghai Animation Film Studios
>
> The Dubbing Film Studio
>
> The Science and Education Film Studios

Elsewhere there are:

> The Pearl River Film Studios, Guangzhou (features only)
>
> The Xi'an Studio, Xi'an
>
> The Changchun Film Studios, Changchun
>
> The Omei Film Studios, Chengtu

The Hohhot Film Studios, Inner Mongolia

Most of the studios have their teams of producers, writers, directors, actors, and so on, and are capable of doing all work from pre- to postproduction. There are, however, several separate organizations that provide support to the industry:

The China Equipment Corporation (advice and research)

The China Film Archives

The Beijing Film Laboratory

The Beijing Film Institute (training for technicians and actors)

The China Film Company for Coproductions (CCCC) (a branch of the Ministry of Foreign Affairs)

The Beijing Academy of Film

The industry is dominated by the two main feature film studios, the Shanghai Film Studios and the Beijing Film Studios. Of the rest, seven produce features and seven produce only specialist (e.g., educational) films. The Shanghai Dubbing Studio is the only exclusively dubbing studio in the country and its 100-strong staff can dub a feature in five days.

The studio most likely to take the leadership in any future development is the Shanghai Film Studios (SFS). Of all China's studios the SFS are the oldest (started in the 1920s) and the largest (1800 workers). In 1977 and 1978 they produced eight features. In 1979 their quota was 12, but by October they had already produced 18. In 1980 their quota is 14, and they are likely to produce considerably more. Of the 1800 workers, 80 are directors and assistant directors and 220 are scriptwriters or actors. A recent innovation is the setting up of five "creative collectives," each with about 20 or 30 workers, who will participate in the planning and making of their films. Even within these collectives (and somewhat surprisingly for China), it is virtually impossible for a director to work as a cameraman, or a cameraman as a director, on a particular film. There is no flexibility of functions between the two grades.

The SFS have six sound stages. The largest is 80 by 120 feet (No. 4); the smallest is 60 by 100 feet (No. 6). All the studios have wooden floors. For one film I saw, a classical opera, a large platform was built, covering the entire floor, so that spots could be hidden between the edge of the platform and the backcloth; a laborious procedure indeed, especially as they were shooting in the round. A classical opera of 100 minutes would expect to be in the studio for about two months, and the material would be edited as shooting progressed. Dialogue would never be recorded at the same time as the visuals, but always added later. Films intended for national distribution are recorded in putonghua; local films in the Shanghai dialect.

Most of the equipment in the SFS is Chinese-made, with the usual exceptions. Most cameras are made in Shanghai (there are some imported Arriflex), and so is most of the ancillary equipment. But the Chinese are not yet confident about optic or magnetic recording. The majority of the lenses are imported (Canon zoom lenses are popular), and all the tape recorders are either Nagra (the most popular) or Studer. Eastman film is produced in Baoding (color and monochrome) and in Shanghai itself (color only).

Most films are shot on location, with sync sound, and only a few studio inserts. The SFS have a tradition of colorful historical adventures, usually based on a true story. I saw extracts from two major products, each budgeted at 2.5 million yuan, "From a Slave to a General," about General Liu Shao, and "Heroine of the North-East," about Aulie Yilan. The studios have an equal reputation for contemporary stories. "The Laughter of a Distressed Man" tells the story of a local journalist who was persecuted by the Gang of Four. The villain of the story is the secretary of the municipal branch of the CCP and the editor of the party newspaper; the character is modeled on the man who actually was in those positions when the Gang of Four held sway.

The second largest film studios are the Beijing Film Studios, which were founded by the CCP when it captured the city in 1949. The studios employ about 1200 people, including 30 directors, 30 assistant directors, and about 110 actors and actresses. There are five stages, some of which could provide sound but have been silent for some time. The studios produced 12 features in 1979 and hoped to produce 15 in 1980 (although the quota for 1980 remained at 12).

The themes of the studios' output for 1980 were described by the head, Wang Yang, in May 1980. He said, "to better serve the country's modernization, the theme of films must be diversified. Though the emphasis should be laid on industrial and agricultural construction and on revolutionary history, there should be some fairy tales and legends, good landscape scenery and some fighting." It is a good summary of Chinese films.

The list of films already planned by Wang Yang actually includes two sagas of revolutionary history, "Oath of a Marshall," about Marshall He Long's struggle against Lin Biao (with Li Rentang, star of "Tearstain," playing the marshall) and "Chen Yi Goes into Action," about the poet and fighter of the 1930s. The studios will also make "Regret for the Past," based on Lu Xun's story about the intellectuals' struggle for freedom in the 1920s and 1930s, and "Peacock Princess," a story by Bai Hua about some "minority" people.

Wages in the Shanghai, Beijing, and other main studios are relatively high. Senior directors may earn 250 yuan a month, with bonuses of one week's wage for a film that is successful at the box office. A medium wage for directors and actors would be about 200 yuan a month.

## DISTRIBUTION AND EXHIBITION

All films produced in China, except the most specialist, are bought by the China Film Corporation for distribution and exhibition. Originally, the CFC paid the studio a fixed price irrespective of the nature of the film; so that a black-and-white short got the same as a color feature. The price was also slightly affected by the film's earnings at the box office. This principle of a flat fee was not exclusive to film. Writers in China get paid a fixed fee according to the number of characters they have written. A famous writer may get no more than an average writer.

This fee structure has been criticized recently as discouraging to all potential writers and unfair to the exceptionally talented. It is true, however, that writers and other intellectuals can have considerable perks. The private life of Cao Yu, by general consent China's greatest living playwright, was described by Fox Butterfield in *The New York Times* (20 February 1980) in these terms: "Mr Cao lives comfortably now (after ten years of arrest during the Cultural Revolution, when he was put to cleaning pigsties), like most other senior intellectuals who are supported by the state. He draws a government salary equivalent to over $200 a month, whereas the average city worker makes under $40 a month and the average peasant less than $60 a year. He has a chauffeur-driven car in a country where there are no private vehicles, and he is known to have a spacious apartment with a private telephone and a house-keeper, also rarities." In 1980, however, the policy of an overall flat fee, with marked exceptions for the famous, will be replaced by a more complicated scheme in which the CFC's fees take into account the cost of the film and its revenue. The new policy clearly gives added force to the filmmaker as professional, as expert.

China has 4500 cinemas throughout the country, all using 35 mm projection. The majority are exclusively used for showing films, but about 1500 are multipurpose places that are also used for theater, meetings, and so forth. Some multipurpose places use 16 mm projectors (a favorite is the new Yangtse River 16 mm projector with mag./opt. sound). Beijing has 26 cinemas and about 70 multipurpose places where films can be shown. Shanghai has about half as many again, as befits its larger population and its historic leadership of the Chinese film industry.

In China, however, the cinema plays only a minor role in the exhibition of film. For the 80 percent of the people who live in the countryside a quite different method is required. China's answer has been the development of film units or projection teams, consisting of one or two people and two projectors. For these teams the film is transferred from 35 mm to 16 mm or to 8.75 mm stock. The 8.75 mm format is a special Chinese innovation, slightly larger than the worldwide standard Super-8. Nevertheless some Super-8 equipment, also made in China, is likely to be introduced in 1980 and will probably supersede the 8.75 mm format.

The CFC reckons there are 110,000 film units in China, of which 90,000 work in the countryside and 20,000 in the towns. The price of admittance to see a film varies from 20–30 cents in the cities down to 10 cents or less in the countryside. Students need pay only 5 cents during the vacation. The numbers of people seeing films in cinemas or other public places is probably greater in China than in any other country. The State Statistical Bureau gave the national total number of admissions in 1979 as 29 billion, an enormous number that means, on average, that each person went to a cinema no less than 29 times. The figure in the Beijing area is even higher, according to the *Beijing Daily* (14 March 1980). The paper reported that "every Beijing peasant attended an average of 52 film shows last year, including Chinese and foreign feature films, documentaries, and scientific and educational news reels (but not including any films shown on TV)." The same report said there were 1500 film projection teams in rural Beijing, and that every commune has one, and some have two. A quarter of the production brigades have their own projection teams. There were only 140 such teams in rural Beijing in 1964, said the report. The figures for Shanghai are equally impressive. In the first half of 1979, according to the CFC, about 900,000 people (8 percent of the population of 11 million) saw a film every day.

An increasingly popular alternative are the movies on television. Astonishingly, the TV stations do not pay CFC or the studios for the films that they transmit. The station simply requests a print from the CFC (requests are always met) and then either uses a telecine or transfers to a U-matic cassette. Most stations transfer to a cassette, which is a severe jump from the original 35 mm print, and transmit direct from that.

In the past there has been little concern about the duplication of films on television and in the cinema. The cinema was seen as the dominant medium, with television as a junior partner. TV sets were scarce and they were mostly black-and-white. But in 1979 the spread of television and the trend towards color sets threatened the cinema's economic and cultural position. After some prolonged discussions, the CFC ruled that, except for public holidays, when one new film would be shown on television, the TV stations should wait six months after the theatrical release before showing a film on television. But this agreement is unlikely to last. The TV stations can quote strong public need, and the principle of a democratic public service, to back their argument that they should show films as they become available. Furthermore, they have a measure of support from the viewers. CCTV received 6000 letters in three months in support of their argument. Against that, the cinemas have found it difficult to substantiate their claims that box office receipts are diminishing. The queues seem as long as ever.

An indication of the kind of films that are most popular with both the studios and the audiences can be got from the Hundred Flowers Awards organized in May by *Dazhong Dianying* ("Popular Movies") magazine. Like so many other events of this kind the Hundred Flowers Awards have just been reinstated after a lengthy disappearance. First held in 1962 and then again in 1963, the awards were not given again until 1980. Partly because of the gap, the third awards generated enormous interest and attracted over 700,000 votes from the magazine's readers. Three films tied for the top award given to the best film made in 1976–1979: "General Ji Hougchang," about a KMT officer who joins the communists to help in the fight against the Japanese in the 1930s; "Tearstain," about a rural CCP official who clears his predecessor of false charges; and "Little Flower," a complex family story, of the kind always beloved by the Chinese, about a reunion between a PLA soldier and his two sisters during the war of Liberation. No film awards are complete without a rumor of bias, and it must be recorded that some people said that "Two Pairs of Twins," a comedy made in Shanghai and using novel split-screen techniques, actually got the largest number of votes. If it did, the reason, on the basis of the rough cut I saw, was its novelty, and nothing else. Of the Hundred Flowers' other awards, the most important were the award of the best actor to Li Rentang, a 50-year-old writer, dramatist, and actor who played the party secretary in "Tearstain," and the award of best actress to Chen Chong, a 19-year-old student, who was chosen to play the lead in "Little Flower." These two performances also won awards from the Ministry of Culture and *Wenwei Bao*, a Shanghai newspaper, in their selections of the best recent films.

In the last few years an ever increasing number of European, U.S., and Canadian film companies have applied to make films in China for distribution at home. Some are easily accommodated, especially TV crews who want or need minimal technical support. It is obviously more difficult to arrange a coproduction. The CFC receives three or four applications a week, and only a very few are accepted. Understandably, the ones with the best chances are those sympathetic to China. The Canada/China coproduction of "Dr. Bethune," which was scheduled to start shooting in March 1981, was accepted because of China's profound reverence for the eponymous Norman Bethune; otherwise, the CCC would have been unlikely to bother with a film that needed 35,000 extras. Other films being coproduced in 1980–1981 include "The Lady and the Panda" (the first USA/China coproduction deal), which is based, like "Dr. Bethune," on a true story, and the massive USA/Italy/China epic, "Marco Polo."

# Chapter 5

## Publishing and Printing

Print is as important to China as it is to any highly bureaucratic, highly dogmatic organization. At the same time, the Chinese face three basic handicaps in exploiting print's potential. Their language is based on characters, many of which are complex and whose pronunciation or meaning have to be learnt one by one. Second, China has a high rate of illiteracy in spite of many energetic campaigns by the CCP to eradicate it. Third, there is the problem, already mentioned, of China's many dialects.

The nature of printing means that it can be carried out with equal efficacy both by large corporations and by small groups of individuals. The diversity of organizations ranges from Xinhua, with computerized setting and eight-color printing, to private hand presses. China tends to favor the former, but the latter do exist.

There are three different sectors: publishing, printing, and distribution. The publishing sector contains 158 registered publishers and an uncountable number of incidental publishers. The printing sector is the most diverse of the three; there are estimated to be some 10,000 printers throughout the country. Bookselling is dominated by the Xinhua chain of shops.

The most popular books are nonfiction (education, science, dictionaries, etc.), but the number of fiction and literary works, both Chinese and foreign, has grown noticeably in the past few years. The staple diet of reprinted classics is being varied increasingly with new works. The proliferation of excellent literary magazines (Shanghai's *Shouhuo*, or "Harvest;" Beijing's *Dangdai*, "Contemporary;" and *Shiyue*, "October"), the greater freedom of publication, and the eagerness of readers have generated an active market in more and longer works.

As well as the Han majority, there are 55 minority languages, spoken by about 24 million people (about 6 percent of the total). Of these, 19 have recognized written languages. At the end of 1980 there were 19 publishers with special departments for minority languages, staffed by about 1000 editors and translators (XHNA, 8 December 1980).

## HISTORY

The Chinese invented printing long before any other nation. They regard it as one of their four great inventions, the others being papermaking, gunpowder, and the compass. The basic formula for ink was discovered around 2000 B.C., while paper, and the notion of relief engraving, were introduced at the end of the Han dynasty in the second century A.D. The first proper invention was of block printing, around 500 B.C., to satisfy the Buddhists' increasing demands for copies of sacred texts. Moveable type (one of the two key inventions normally ascribed to Johannes Gutenberg) was first used in the eleventh century. In A.D. 1313 a magistrate called Wang Chen had 60,000 moveable characters manufactured so that he could write a treatise on, appropriately, the history of technology. But the Chinese never developed the other key device, the printing press, and they lacked the suitable economic and cultural environment to develop further in their own manner.

The history of Chinese printing and publishing is inextricably a part of the rich tapestry of Chinese literature. But here is not the place to recount the twists and turns of that intricate art. Suffice it to say that for many centuries the printing and publishing industries were intimately linked to, and dependent on, the various imperial and court notions of civilization and art. With the emergence of the communists, the workers had another code, utterly different, but just as rigid, to govern their actions.

The history of modern printing (or, as the communists say, "printing for the masses") began officially as far back as the 4 May Movement, which was a nationalist, but not KMT Nationalist, reaction to the 1919 Versailles Treaty. The following year Mao Tsetung established an organization called the Cultural Book Society, which undertook a variety of tasks including the printing and distributing of propaganda; it also printed revolutionary literature. During the twenties the nascent CCP continued to use print as an essential support for its revolutionary activities. In the late thirties the party set up the first Xinhua Bookstore in Yanan, the town in Shaanxi from which Mao directed his battles against the Nationalists and the Japanese. The name was symbolic — "New China" — and during the forties was adopted by all the communist printing works, publishers, and bookshops. From 1940 to Liberation, according to the official statistics, the Xinhua network produced some 5300 titles, of which some 44 million copies were distributed.

After Liberation the Xinhua sectors of publishing, printing, and distribution were quickly consolidated and expanded. The State Publications Administration (SPA) was appointed to be the coordinating body and, to some extent, to act as the regulatory agency. From 1949 to 1978, again according to official statistics, some 295,000 titles were published, of which 53,960 million copies were sold. The figures for 1979 were expected to reach record levels for titles and copies.

The publishing business was greatly affected, of course, by the Great Leap Forward and the Cultural Revolution. Each time, the CCP used its print resources to the maximum. In the middle of the Great Leap Forward, for instance, the Shanghai publishing organizations managed to print 24 million copies of the *General Line of Socialist Construction* in just two months.

Since 1976 the print industries have expanded in many directions. The number of publishers has increased and is still increasing (103 in mid-1978, 158 by the end of 1980) and their work now encompasses complicated technical texts, and diagrams, excellent color reproduction, and the printing of foreign journals for distribution within China. A symbol of the new age is the computer typesetting system installed in Beijing and Shanghai by Monotype, which can set and edit ideographic type with astonishing ease.

The three sectors are cross-divided here into national and regional organizations. The national are dominated and regulated by the State Publications Administration. The regional ones are regulated by the authorities of the relevant provincial, municipal, and autonomous regions. Most Chinese publishing has traditionally been centered in Beijing, but by 1979 the number of publishers and printers was fairly evenly split between the capital and the rest of the country (a split which still gave Beijing a much higher per-capita figure). The trend for the future is almost certainly for print activities to expand much faster in the provinces than in the capital.

## THE STATE PUBLICATIONS ADMINISTRATION

The State Publications Administration (SPA) is the senior regulatory body for printing, publishing, and distribution. As an agency of the State Council it has a status practically equivalent to that of a ministry. Two other organizations are also responsible for print. The Ministry of Culture has an overall responsibility for all things cultural and is concerned with strategies and planning. Second, the Propaganda Committee of the CCP Central Committee has considerable influence not only in the SPB (and the ministry) but in all component units of the industry. The three organizations can be distinguished by saying that the Ministry of Culture is concerned with overall policy, the Propaganda Committee with the ideological aspects, and the SPB with the task of knitting the two strands into a set of plans that can be and will be carried out by individual publishers and printers.

The SPA regulates the industry in two ways. It works through policies and might, for instance, issue a policy statement on the relationship between costs and prices. It also controls through executive action. For instance, it orders and distributes all supplies of paper to the publishers under its control (who then allocate their quota to the printers). In 1979 it supplied 500,000 tons of paper.

## PUBLISHING: BOOKS

In Chinese parlance, the term *publisher* is restricted to an organization that is registered to publish books and periodicals. At the end of 1980 there were 158 organizations registered to publish books: about 60 in Beijing, 15 in Shanghai, and 80 in the rest of the country. At the national level, there are ten specialized publishers directly under the SPA:

The People's Publishing House (works by Marx, Engels, Stalin, Mao Tsetung, state documents, etc.)

Sanlian Bookstore (social sciences)

The Commercial Press (reference books, social sciences in both Chinese and foreign languages)

Zhong Hua Publishing House (classical works)

The People's Literature Publishing House (Chinese and foreign literature)

The People's Fine Art Publishing House

The People's Music Publishing House

The China Encyclopaedia

The Chinese Photography Publications House (photography of China)

The Beijing Braille Publishing House (braille texts for the blind)

There are about 50 other specialist publishers, which are regulated, in varying ways, by the SPA (albeit minimally), the CCP, the State Council and its ministries, and so on. The major ones are:

The Science Press (science textbooks; a part of Academis Sinica)

The Foreign Language Press (the source of virtually all foreign language books and periodicals in general distribution; set up in 1952)

The China Youth Publishing House

The People's Education Publishing House

The Cartographic Publishing House (maps and charts)

The People's Physical Cultural Publishing House (sports, etc.)

The Social Sciences Publishing House (under the Chinese Academy of Social Sciences)

At the regional level, there are about 80 publishers. Most are general publishers, in the Chinese, not the Western sense of the term (i.e., nonspecialist). They are regulated by the appropriate regional or local Propaganda Committee of the CCP.

The number of books published is increasing rapidly. In 1978, according to the SPA, about 15,000 books were published (half in Beijing). The total number of copies printed was about 3000 million, giving an average print run of 200,000 per book. The 1979 figures rose to 17,000 titles and 4200 million copies (a somewhat lower figure of 4070 million copies had been given earlier by the SPA, presumably before all the returns were in).

## PERIODICALS

China has a strong national and regional press. The total number of national and regional newspapers in 1979 was 1200, an increase of 450 over the 1976 figure, while circulation figures had increased by 44 percent since that year (*Beijing Review*, 4 February 1980). The total seems to be continually rising and by the end of 1980 had reached 1700 with a total circulation of 150 million (*Beijing Review*, 20 October 1980).

The country's major newspaper is *Renmin Ribao*

("People's Daily"), which is published by the CCP Central Committee in Beijing and other main cities. Its circulation of 6–7 million copies a day makes it the best-selling newspaper in the country, although some of the Xinhua News Agency's "internal" bulletins have a wider distribution; according to *Beijing Review* (4 February 1980), the *Cankao Xiaoxo* ("Foreign News Bulletin") prints as many as 9 million copies every day. A Hong Kong edition of *Renmin Ribao* is printed and distributed by Wen Wei Po. The text is transmitted from Beijing to Guangzhou to Hong Kong by facsimile, printed at the Wen Wei Po works and sold in Hong Kong and Macao.

There are several other national newspapers, of which the dominant one is probably *Gongren Ribao* ("Workers Daily") which is published by the All China Federation of Trade Unions in Beijing, and *Jiefang Ribao* ("Liberation Daily") which is published in both Beijing and Shanghai by the CCP Military Commission. *Zhongguo Qingnian Bao* ("China Youth News") is published by the Communist Youth News on Tuesdays, Thursdays, and Saturdays. All the rest are published daily, except for *Gongren Ribao* which doesn't appear on Mondays.

All the major regional capitals also have their own daily newspaper, with circulations around the million mark (the shortage of newsprint often inhibits further growth). The main ones are *Beijing Ribao, Guangzhou Ribao, Tianjin Ribao*, Shanghai's *Wen Hui Bao* and *Hopei Ribao*. Many newspapers are starting evening and regional editions. The *Beijing Wanba* ("Evening News") resumed publication in February 1980 after a break of some 13 years. Later the same year, in September, a four-page countryside edition of *Beijing Ribao* began to be published twice a week for distribution in the nearby towns and communes.

Probably the fastest moving sector of Chinese publishing at the moment is the magazine. In 1978 some 890 magazines were readily available, and they sold a total of 760 million copies. In 1979 the number of titles rose to 1200, and the number of copies sold reached 1180 million. They ranged from *Nongye Jishu* ("Agricultural Technology") to *Dazhong Dianying* ("Popular Movies") which sells 2 million copies. Several TV stations publish their own "TV Guide" (e.g., Shanghai's *Meizhou Guangbo Dianshi*). A magazine on radio techniques, *Wuxiandian*, sells 1.3 million copies every month. The best selling periodical of all is *Red Flag*, the CCP's own magazine, of which 9.7 million copies are distributed. Another popular magazine is *Zhongguo Shaonian Bao* ("Chinese Children's News") which sells 7 million copies.

Specialist magazines include *Dianying Jishu* (film technology), *Huashi* (fossils), *Huaxue Tongbao* (chemistry bulletin), *Xuebao* (journal of construction engineering), *Kexue Shiyan* (scientific experiments), *Shuxe de Shixien yu Renshi* (journal of mathematical theory and applied mathematics), *Shuxue Xuebao* (journal of mathematics), *Renmin Wenxue* (people's literature), *Wenhua yu Shenghuo* (culture and life), *Wuli* (physics), *Xin Tiyu* (sports), *Yichuan* (genetics), *Zhongguo Kexue* (Chinese science), *Zhongguo Sheying* (Chinese photography), *Zhonghua Erke Zazhi* (Chinese pediatrics), *Zhonghua Fuchanke Zazhi* (Chinese gynaecology), *Zhonghua Neike Zazhi* (Chinese internal medicine), *Zhonghua Shenjing Jingsheke Zazhi* (Chinese neurology and mental disorders).

China also publishes six magazines in foreign languages. They are *China Pictorial* (which, uniquely among the six, has a Chinese language edition which sells 900,000 copies); *Beijing Review*, a political weekly; *China Reconstructs*, monthly general news and features; *Chinese Literature*, monthly, original writing and criticism; *People's China*, monthly, Japan only; and *El Popola Cinio*, monthly, Esperanto only.

## PRINTING

There are about 8000 printers in China, according to the State Publications Administration. Of these, only 210 are registered to print books and magazines; the remainder are general printers of stationery, leaflets, posters, tickets, and so on. Only a few printers (23 out of the 210) are in Beijing, the bulk are distributed throughout the rest of the country. The largest printer is the Xinhua Printing Works in Beijing which has 3800 workers. The average plant has between 500 and 1500 workers.

The diversity of the work means that it is difficult to generalize about the type (and age) of machinery in use; about the types, weights, and so forth of paper, and the ease with which a production manager can obtain the paper he wants; about the quality of ink; and so on. At Xinhua Printing Works, Beijing, the Commercial Press, Shanghai, and in Tianjin, which has the great asset of the Light Industry Research Institute of Paper Technology, the equipment and techniques are relatively modern. Elsewhere, standards are lower. A major obstacle to the development of quality printing for the domestic market is the chronic shortage of disposable income on the part of individuals and organizations. The retail prices of books and magazines have to be kept to a minimum; there is no latent demand for more expensive books.

The Xinhua Printing Works, in the suburbs of Beijing, is the largest and most modern in China. It has seven divisions for general books and magazines, and two for illustrated work. The great majority of its output is books and magazines, but it also produces some calendars and brochures (of considerable quality). At present, all typesetting is done by hand, although alternatives are being explored and tested. The 200 compositors sit in bays holding about 3000 characters of the typeface being used and can generally set about 10,000 characters in an eight-hour day. No more than 20 fonts are in regular use. The most popular size for books is 10pt, usually set with 12pt leading.

The complexity of the Chinese script has long prevented the use of a keyboard and any form of mechanical setting. However, two alternatives to hand setting are being actively investigated by the Xinhua Printing Works. The simpler system is a grid device which the operator uses to throw a beam of light on to the required character, which is then set on paper. Much more significant is the Monotype Ideographic Lasercomp Photo-typesetting System which Monotype installed in Beijing and Shanghai at the end of 1980. The system uses keyboards, computers, lasers, and video displays to set, display, print on tape, edit, and produce repro. Its breakthrough is the use of a keyboard to set Chinese characters. It is the first system to reduce the components of the characters to a form which is amenable to keyboard instructions. The principle is simple: each character is broken down into key components. On average, the compositor needs 2.7 strokes to construct a character.

The Beijing system has several LD-400 keyboards, each with 255 keys. Each keyboard's output can be recorded on disc (capable of holding 70,000 characters) or on punched tape. The tape can then be fed into the Laser Compositor (Lasercomp). Naturally any tape can be fed into the Lasercomp, and in fact, the Lasercomp in Shanghai can communicate directly with the Lasercomp in Beijing. The Lasercomp then prints the information (the desired characters, etc.) either on paper or on film. On the first cycle, the operator will usually request paper so that he or she can check the setting, make author's corrections, proof the text, and so forth. All these corrections will be done on a computerized editing terminal, which, again, can produce either paper, for more proofing, or discs. Eventually, when all is correct, the Lasercomp will produce repro for the artwork. Monotype and the Xinhua Printing Works have combined to design a special face for their system. The font ranges from 5 pt to 96 pt, in roman, italic, and bold. The first Chinese-language book to be set by the Monotype Lasercomp — indeed, the first Chinese language book to be set by a computerized photosetter — was *How It Works ... The Computer* (Ladybird), which Xinhua printed in Beijing.

Xinhua has some difficulty in obtaining the right supplies of the right paper at the right time; partly because, in printing so much color work, its needs are for the high-quality, heavy art papers that China finds difficult to manufacture. The bulk of its paper is Chinese-made and comes from the Ministry of Light Industries according to the allocation made by the State Publications Administration. Imports come either through the China National Import/Export Corporations or, increasingly, direct to the works. The most common paper used by Xinhua for book printing is 60/70 gsm. All the ink used by Xinhua is made in China.

Most of the machinery is old and old-fashioned. The presses tend to be imported. Makes include Webor, the Polygraph PET 6 rotary press, the Plamag 8-color system from West Germany, and a Roland-Ultra offset-lithography press, which prints four colors on 4500 sheets an hour. However, China does make some fairly modern presses. The Hunan Printing Machine Factory is producing an automatic single-color offset press which can print 7000 pages an hour, on a maximum page area of 480 × 660 mm (the J4103). But China's main contribution to printing machinery is in the support areas of folding, cutting, binding, and sewing. All Xinhua's ancillary equipment is Chinese-made.

The first foreign periodical to be printed in China in the Chinese language was *Scientific American* (or *Ke Xue*, as it is known). By 1979 *Scientific American* had established five non-USA editions, in France, Italy, Spain, West Germany, and Japan, and the publisher began to look towards a Chinese-language edition. They soon discovered that the Chinese, so to speak, had beaten them to it. The Chinese Institute for Scientific and Technological Information had been reprinting the English-language version for four or five years and, since January 1979, they had even been translating the English version into their own Chinese version. Unabashed, the two sides agreed to proceed on more formal terms.

## DISTRIBUTION

The most visible evidence of the print boom in China is the long queues that one sees outside a bookshop whenever a new book or a new series is published. Bookshops sometimes stay open throughout the night to cope with demands. The distribution of books in China is administered by the Xinhua Shudian ("New China Bookstore"). It has its headquarters in Beijing and 5000 branches in towns and villages. The central office is responsible, under the Ministry of Culture, for the distribution (storage, invoicing, sales, etc.) of all books produced by the national publishers and for coordinating sales of books produced at the regional level. It has major regional subsidiaries in Beijing and Shanghai to liaise with the many publishers in each city. In 1980 Beijing had 105 bookshops. The year's best sellers, according to regular reports in *Beijing Review*, were science, university teaching materials, Chinese and world classics, and dictionaries. Each bookshop is seen as a profit center and has to fulfill a quota for sales, revenue, and expenditure. Profits are taxed; the tax rates are higher for urban sites than for country sites. Prices are low, with an average of one yuan or less, although dictionaries are typically 5–6 yuan. Most bookshops also operate a "reading room," where people can browse, and a more formal library, where they can borrow books.

A separate network is operated by the Waiwen Shudian ("Foreign Languages Bookstore"). It has outlets in all major cities. Magazines and newspapers are also sold by the post office. It is possible to read most magazines for two hours for half the cover price. Special rooms are reserved for this purpose.

In October 1979 the Beijing Xinhua bookshop held a ten-day book fair. It was the first time since 1957 that the fair had been held. Among the notable writers who attended were Ding Ling, Xie Bingxin, and He Jinzhi. One writer, Zhang Kejia, recalled how, during the Cultural Revolution, his poetry had been sold for 14 cents a kilo, for waste paper. The fair sold 400,000 books on the first day, from a selection of 6000 titles. Among the foreign titles on offer were Balzac, Maupassant, Moliere, Chekhov, Dickens, Dumas, Hugo, Shakespeare, Defoe, and Gorky. At a second National Book Fair in October 1980 over 100 publishers displayed some 12,000 books at a massive two-week event in the Cultural Palace of the Working People. Over 700,000 people attended and bought a total of 6 million books (*Beijing Review*, 17 November 1980). Several foreign fairs have been held in China. The first, an international fair, was held in Beijing in 1978. The first national fair was organized by the UK Publishers' Association later the same year; the association held its second fair in November 1979 in Beijing and other cities. West Germany held a fair in April 1979, and Japan in August. Australia, France, and the USA held fairs in 1980.

All Chinese publications are exported by an organization called the Guozi Shudian (China Publications Center). Guozi Shudian also exports newspapers, periodicals, pictures, postcards, paper cuts, and records.

The China National Publications Import Corporation

has a monopoly of imported books and periodicals. Senpik-corp, as it is known, currently imports about 10,000 magazines: 2000 from the UK, 4000 from continental Western Europe, and 3000 from the USA. Its main clients are libraries, institutes, academics, universities, and the government. Individuals can order titles, but the shortage of foreign currency and the expense of foreign books restricts most orders to organizations. Orders are processed and books distributed through 28 Foreign Language Distribution Centers.

# Chapter 6

## Telecommunications: From Beacon Fires to Satellites

China has long been aware of the importance of good public communications. In the early years of the Han dynasty, the government used fires to send messages. Later, the canals provided an alternative network. In more modern times, the Chinese, like every other nation, put up wires alongside the railway tracks to send telegraphs. In 1882 the government established the Chinese Telegraph Administration. At the turn of the twentieth century it started telephone and then radio (wireless) services.

Nowadays, the most efficient means of establishing a national communications network is by electronics — by telecommunications. A telephone system is an excellent way of talking, listening, monitoring, informing — especially across vast distances. To begin with, it can provide telephone links; later, it can be used for telex, facsimile, and more.

For some years, in the words of Yu Qiuli at the second session of the Fifth National People's Congress, China's telecommunications services have been in "a strained situation." But that may be changing.

The central regulatory agency for the public switched network is the Ministry of Posts and Telecommunications (PTT). The party organization most closely involved is the Department of Industry and Communications, an agency of the CCP Central Committee. In recent years the Ministry of Posts and Telecommunications has consolidated and centralized its authority over all levels of the country's networks.

The PTT has 13 departments: the general office, the directorate of posts, the directorate of telecommunications, the department of external affairs, the department of personnel, the department of education, the department of planning, the department of finance, the department of industrial management, the deparment of supplies, the department of capital construction, the department of maintenance, and the department of science and technology. The PTT has a total of 700,000 workers, distributed in 50,000 offices throughout the country. In 1979 its national turnover was 1255 million yuan, an increase of 7.7 percent over the 1978 figure (XHNA, 30 April 1980).

China has 3.7 million telephones, excluding "private" networks operated by the military, railways, and so on. It is a tiny total for a country with a population of over 950 million. Practically all telephones are installed in places of work. Sometimes, a senior official will also have a telephone in his or her home. It is practically impossible to obtain a private telephone unless it is judged to be in the public's interest. In the towns, there are many phones in flats and so on. The worse shortage is in the countryside, where 80 percent of the population have only 50 percent of the telephones. All communes have a telephone, but only

70–80 percent of production brigades and only 60 percent of production teams are so fortunate.

The majority of telephone exchanges are step-by-step. Crossbar exchanges, which are rapidly becoming obsolete in the West, were introduced in China only a few years ago. The ministry is now investigating semi- and full-electronic exchanges, with stored program control (SPC), the installation of which would be a big jump forward.

Local calls are always free. As for other calls, tariffs are fixed by the relevant authority of the municipal, provincial, or autonomous region. In addition, there is an installation charge, and a monthly rental which varies between 6 and 15 yuan. In 1978 the network arranged 570 million trunk connections and 127 million telegrams.

The transmission network mainly consists of open wires (usually iron) with 1, 3, or 12 carrier systems. Several microwave links have been installed, with capacities between 60 and 960 channels. In addition, some coaxial links have been laid, including an 1800-channel cable between Beijing, Shanghai, and Guangzhou. In 1976 an undersea cable between China and Japan became operational, with 480 voice circuits.

Most of the network is old and primitive, but there are exceptions. International connections are excellent. And Shanghai even has an optic fiber link, a 1.8-kilometer circuit between the Sichuan Road and Haining Road exchanges. So far, its capacity is limited. But the existence of something as sophisticated as an optic fiber system, in full working order, is another revealing insight into the progress made by China, even during the depredations of the Gang of Four, on some very advanced kinds of technology.

Fiber optics rate with satellites as one of the most important communication devices of the future. The strands of glass (thin as a human hair and just as bendy) are considerably more efficient, more capacious, and soon expected to be much cheaper, than copper wiring or coaxial cable. There's no doubt that every country wishing to expand its telephone and TV networks would favor optic fibers over the traditional materials. But most countries are stuck with huge investments in their existing systems. China has no such problem.

The Shanghai link has a capacity of 300 channels, of which 120 are operational. It provides 8.448 megabits per second. The Chinese say attentuation is between 3 and 7 decibels per kilometer. The bit rate is sufficient for telephone calls, telex, facsimile, and so on, but not for television. The fiber doesn't compare with British Telecom's link between Hitchin and Stevenage, installed in 1977 (and claimed to be the world's first operational link). The British link has a capacity of 140 megabits per second, more than sufficient for color video. But the lower rates are perfectly adequate for voice and data. British Telecom's plans for its next 15 links, starting next year, include ten at 8 megabits per second.

The Chinese have developed the technology of optic fibers, and manufactured the fiber, virtually without outside help, although they have received foreign trade delegations, and traveled to fiber optic research centers in Japan and elsewhere. The theoretical work was done by the Chinese Academy of Sciences and in Shanghai's own universities. The main problem, according to the Shanghai 519 Factory which manufactured the fiber, is the operating life of the light-emitting diode that provides the light source. Other similar systems, based on Shanghai's work, have been installed in Peking and Hunan; each, like Shanghai's, on one year's trial. The most likely next step is for Shanghai to install a longer link of 5–7 kilometers with the same bit rate. Next come higher bit rates, in the internationally agreed steps of 34 and 140.

## SATELLITES

Around the world the terrestrial innovation of fiber optic links is being matched in space by the development of communications satellites. Satellites and their ground stations are popular symbols of modern China. Images of satellites in flight can be seen everywhere, on posters, notebooks, factory notice boards, and the covers of fashionable science magazines (usually with realistic but incorrect vapor trails). Many visitors are surprised that China has satellites at all. Even experts have been surprised at the extent to which China has developed, manufactured, and operated satellite systems with virtually no help from foreign countries.

The reason is largely China's requirement for an independent system of nuclear weaponry, at a time when it was not able to make any agreements with any of the world's suppliers of such things. (China exploded its first nuclear bomb in 1964.) Moreover, China has a strong mission of self-reliance, as we have seen. The result is that China now has a substantial space industry. The desire for modernization and the policy to extend the telecommunications network as rapidly as possible mean that China is also shopping for satellites for domestic communications.

China built and launched its first satellite in 1970. The Tung Fang Hung circled the Earth transmitting the revolutionary song, "The East is Red." The satellite was developed by the National Academy of Space Technology, which had been set up two years earlier. See table 6.1.

In 1972, in the circumstances of President Nixon's visit, China acquired an RCA ground station which enabled it to send and receive signals (TV, audio, data) to and from the Intelsat system of international communications satellites. Since then, more stations have been bought from Western Union and RCA, and China can now link directly

**Table 6.1 Chinese Satellite Program**

| Name | Date of Launch | International No. | Mass (kg) | Comments |
|---|---|---|---|---|
| China 1 | 1970 (24 April) | 1970-34-A | 173 | Communications satellite, at 20 MHz |
| China 2 | 1971 (3 March) | 1971-18-A | 221 | Experiments in monitoring and surveillance |
| China 3 | 1975 (26 July) | 1975-70-A | 3500 | Similar (decayed 14 September 1975) |
| China 4 | 1975 (26 November) | 1975-111-A | 3500 | Reconnaissance (recovered 2 December 1975) |
| China 5 | 1975 (16 December) | 1975-119-A | 3500 | Meteorological, reconnaissance (recovered 27 January 1976) |
| China 6 | 1976 (30 August) | 1976-87-A | 220 | Scientific experiments (recovered 4 February 1978) |
| China 7 | 1976 (7 December) | 1976-117-A | 3½ tonnes | Reconnaissance (recovered 10 December 1976) |
| China 8 | 1978 (24 January) | 1978-11-A | | Reconnaissance (recovered 7 February 1978) |
| STW-1 | (?) | none | 900 (?) | Communications satellite |
| STW-2 | (?) | none | 900 (?) | Communications satellite |

with Intelsat satellites above the Pacific and Indian Oceans. In October 1980 Fujian province announced a plan to build a satellite ground station (XHNA, 2 October 1980).

In 1978 China signed cooperation agreements with the U.S. National Aeronautics and Space Administration (NASA) and the European Space Agency (ESA).

The Chinese space program is now administered by the National Academy of Space Technology (NAST). The NAST develops the space segments and arranges the launches. The operational work, including the management of the ground stations, is done by the Ministry of Posts and Telecommunications and any relevant agency. For instance, meteorological satellites will be partly the responsibility of the General Meteorological Bureau (an agency of the State Council). The use of a communications satellite to distribute TV programs will likewise involve the Central Broadcasting Administration. Technical collaboration is provided by the Committee on Space Science and Technology, a branch of the Chinese Academy of Science.

The National Academy of Space Technology has 8500 workers, of which 3500 are scientists and engineers. It consists mostly of five institutes and three factories:

> The Beijing Institute of Control Engineering
>
> The Xi'an Radio Technology Institute (research on transponders, antennas, etc.)
>
> The Physics Institute, in Gansu, (a unit involved in system design configuration)
>
> The Beijing Scientific Instrument Factory (assembly and tests)
>
> The Shanghai Scientific Instrument Factory
>
> The Shanxi Taihua Scientific Factory (telemetry)

It also has a research center specifically for communications satellites and a test center for environmental simulation.

The academy's main concern at the moment is the planning and development of a national communications satellite to provide national telecommunications services. Such a satellite would provide substantial capacity for telephone, telex, facsimile, and so on. It would supplement existing terrestrial links and provide other links where none exist. China has already carried out some experiments with the Symphonie satellite operated by France and West Germany, and with the Sakura satellite owned by Japan.

The satellite will be China's first in the Fixed Satellite Service, the International Telecommunication Union's category of fixed telecommunications satellites. Even more important, it will be the country's first satellite to be positioned in the geostationary orbit. All China's satellites so far have had elliptical orbits, with the result that their coverage or beam is continuously moved over the surface of the Earth. This kind of orbit is useful for some kinds of work, but it cannot provide the regular links required for telecommunications services. The answer is to have a satellite in a geostationary (or geosynchronous) orbit. A satellite positioned in this orbit (some 22,300 miles, or 35,900 kilometers, above the equator) travels at such a speed, relative to the Earth, which is also moving, that it remains above the same spot on Earth; in other words, it appears to be stationary. The geostationary orbit is used for all modern communications satellites (except the USSR's Orbita system, which has an elliptical orbit in order to better cover the country).

China has already registered two positions on the geostationary orbit with the International Telecommunication Union (ITU), the United Nations' agency that regulates these matters. Its positions are 125° east and 70° east. It had originally requested 140° east, but Japan asked first. China also has 90° east.

The satellite will send and receive signals from relatively large, "fixed" ground stations. It will operate in the "C" band, with up-links in the 6 GHz band and downlinks in the 4 GHz band. China plans to procure its first fixed satellite for launching in the mid 1980s. At present, it plans to use its own launcher, Long March No. 3, but the satellite is likely to be compatible with both the NASA launchers (the Delta series and the Space Shuttle) and the European Space Agency's Ariane rocket.

China's second priority is a broadcasting satellite. The aim is to have a geostationary satellite capable of broadcasting TV and radio programs direct to community receivers. Without doubt, such a satellite is the quickest and cheapest method of achieving virtually saturation coverage.

It is possible that China will actually build a system that provides both services (following the lead of Canada and, to a lesser extent, India). It has put out tenders for a domestic satellite broadcast and communications system. The system would consist of one operational satellite and one in-orbit spare, with possibly another spare on the ground. They should be compatible for launching either with a Thor Delta class rocket or the Space Shuttle, in the late 1980s. There would be one TT & C (control) station, using the 4/6 GHz band, one mobile transmitter, and a yet-to-be-determined number of receive-only stations.

Each satellite will provide one color TV channel for each of the country's two time zones; three sound channels for the whole country; 3000 telephone channels; a "combined signal of sound broadcasting programs, occupying 240 MHz"; one 9 KHz link, and a service, voice-only channel. The TV and radio signals would use the 12/14 GHz band (the "K" band).

The most likely suppliers of the satellites and associated equipment are Messerschmitt-Bölkow-Blohm of West Germany, with whom China already has some kind of agreement of collaboration (descriptions of its validity vary greatly), or one of several U.S. manufacturers. The latter is the favorite bet, because the Chinese would then have access to other American technologies.

A third development is remote sensing. The technique of using satellites for remote sensing has been vigorously pursued by the USA. The satellites (in a polar orbit) use a variety of sensing devices to take images of the Earth's terrain. It is possible, by means of careful computerized processing of the resulting data, to discover the location and extent of mineral resources, the health of crops, and so on; obviously, this information can have enormous commercial value. Under the U.S.-China Agreement on Cooperation in Science and Technology, which was signed by Vice Premier Deng Xiaoping and President Jimmy Carter on 31 January 1979, the Chinese are currently negotiating the purchase of a Landsat ground station from the USA, which will enable them to receive data from NASA's two operational Landsat satellites. The Chinese are themselves well advanced in these matters: "China has since 1974 developed multispectral scanners, multispectral cameras, microwave radiometers, color compositors, density slicers and acquired some technical know-how on processing and analyzing Landsat imageries and data" (*Beijing Review*, 16 June 1980). The Chinese also want to collaborate with France in its development of the SPOT remote sensing satellite. Ultimately, the Chinese expect to launch and operate their own remote sensing satellite.

Finally, China has not ignored its own development of the important ground segment, the Earth station. It has developed a receive-only satellite Earth station, called Panda, which can receive signals in the 12 GHz band. The antenna is 3.2 meters in diameter, with a gain of 49.5 dB. It weighs 350 kg.

China's future plans are being watched with keen interest by the world's telecommunications manufacturers. It has been suggested that China may soon place contracts with foreign countries that will rival the massive contracts recently signed by the governments of Egypt and Saudi Arabia. Certainly China's size and acknowledged needs might indicate rich pickings. China has already signed a space cooperation agreement with France (her first with a foreign country). Furthermore she has excellent credit facilities. But will China rush to import whole packages of systems?

The expressed policy is to be self-sufficient in all telecommunications equipment. Already, in fact, China is trying to export switching systems. It is selling an HJ-905 crossbar exchange in two sizes, one for 200–400 lines and one for 600–800 lines. The smaller JH 800 PABX has five external lines and 26 extensions. It has also produced a push-button telephone (the ND 868-1), which automatically redials if the number is engaged. She is therefore much more likely to put most effort into technical exchanges, to import only a few key components, and to purchase outright only those items that are desperately urgent and impossible to be Chinese-made.

China became a member of the Universal Postal Union in 1971 and of the International Telecommunication Union in May 1972, following the expulsion of Taiwan.

# Chapter 7

# Advertising

One of the most obvious and, to many people, the most startling, aspects of China's modernization is the rush of advertising that appeared during 1979. In fact, China's first advertising agency, the Shanghai Advertising and Packaging Corporation, was set up in 1962. It kept busy promoting national products, and by advising on the packaging of products for exports. The Cultural Revolution was thoroughly opposed to such activities, however, and the corporation ceased to function until 1978 when it rose again as the Shanghai Advertising Corporation. By the end of 1980 media that did not accept advertising were the exception rather than the rule. Advertising agencies had been set up in Guangzhou, Shangdong, Qingdao, Nanjing, Dalian, Tianjin, and Zhejiang.

The purpose of advertising in China, as far as the

advertiser is concerned, is generally the same as in other national economies: to increase awareness of the product or service, to increase sales, and to maintain market share. For the foreign buyer, increasing awareness is especially important.

The bulk of foreign advertising has been selling products that are not yet available. Television is being used to persuade a few key buyers that they should allow certain goods to be imported. The motives of the seller of the air time or space are not so easily summarized. The main reason is the socialist one of promoting trade in the interest of the four modernizations (of agriculture, industry, national defense, and science and technology).

The second reason is to tap a new source of revenue. However, the extent to which this new revenue will be allowed to be added to existing revenue, rather than replace it, will vary enormously from outlet to outlet.

In China, as elsewhere, both media and message are subject to numerous restrictions. However, there is no central body or even regional body with the responsibility for regulating advertisements or vetting their contents. For instance, the Shanghai Advertising Corporation will not allow alcohol to be advertised on the city's street posters. But Guangzhou Television Station accepts TV ads for alcohol, cigarettes, and medicine without any of the conditions that face Western advertisers in most of their domestic markets.

The three China state agencies qualified to act for Chinese media are the Shanghai Advertising Corporation, the Beijing Advertising Corporation, and the China Advertising Company. The Shanghai Advertising Corporation is the senior organization and handles Shanghai media. The Beijing Advertising Corporation is a newcomer and details are unclear, and advertising in Beijing is still very rare. It is probably intending to act for Beijing media as Shanghai acts for its media. The third agency, the China Advertising Company, is also a state-owned organization and is located in Hong Kong. It acts both as an agency for the Shanghai and Beijing agencies and as an agent in its own right.

A second tier of agencies is composed of three private agencies outside the PRC, which have direct agreements with those within it. All three agencies are in Hong Kong: the Robert Chua group of companies, Wen Wei Po, and McCann Erikson Matheson. The first pair are well established Hong Kong companies. The third was formed in 1979 by McCann Erikson and Jardine Matheson specifically to provide ad services in China. A third tier is composed of agencies in New York, London, Tokyo, and so on, who have agreements of varying kinds to represent the Chinese or Hong Kong agencies.

The competition for the rights to represent a Chinese agency is intense. So far, none of the Chinese agencies have made any agreement beyond allowing foreign agencies, on a nonexclusive basis, to seek business. Advertisers in foreign countries should question any suggestion that an agency has an exclusive deal.

The turnover of ad revenue in China is very small at the moment because all the agencies are still establishing the ground rules and there is considerable confusion about rates and technical specifications. Visitors to Canton who see numerous hoardings should realize that they are looking at a phenomenon which exists only in Guangzhou and Shanghai, and only there in very limited quantities. If one realizes how momentous a change is the introduction of advertising, one can accept that the change must take time.

Statistics on audiences, readerships, pass-on rates, and so forth, do not exist. There is no way of discovering the size of a TV audience within a particular area, or at a particular time of day. One Hong Kong agency has said that

70–80 percent of the people in Sichuan watch TV regularly. I would suggest that 70–80 percent of the Sichuanese may have seen TV but once in their lives.

The readership of a publication is equally difficult to ascertain. The nearest reliable figure is the number of copies that are distributed by the Post Office; in most cases, this figure is significantly less than that in popular use. Pass-on rates are usually held to be very high; up to 50 or even more. The figures are believable for some of the technical periodicals, although probably not as common as often assumed.

Another problem is that the willingness of TV stations and publishers to accept ads is not yet matched by their professional competence. Foreign companies who wish to advertise would do well to be cautious. It would be unwise not to use the Hong Kong agencies, who can speak Chinese (the China Advertising Company's rate card is glossy and smart but entirely in Chinese) and who are quickly accumulating expertise in advertising in China. So far, the business is very informal and done largely on personal contact.

## The Media

The first Chinese broadcasting station to accept commercial advertising was the Shanghai Television Station in February 1979. In theory, anyway. The station did not actually transmit its first ad until 1 November 1979; the gap is a measure of the difficulties to be overcome. By the beginning of December 1979, the regional television stations in Beijing, Shanghai, Guangzhou, Nanjing, and Chengtu, and CCTV's Channel 8 were accepting ads, and others followed during 1980.

The rates are variable and negotiable. A 30-second slot on Beijing Television Station can cost £900–1500 for foreign ads and 180–300 yuan for a Chinese ad. Substantial discounts are available for series and for ads that are not fixed to a specific program. The station has no limit on the number of ads screened per hour, nor on the number of advertising minutes per hour. As for content, each ad is judged separately. Straightforward technical ads have the best chance of success.

The Shanghai Television Station usually charges £900 for 30 seconds with loadings up to 50 percent for special slots. Prices to Chinese organizations are lower. At present, the station is transmitting ads on Channel 5 for about 3–5 minutes per day. In Guangzhou, a 30-second slot costs £450–550 for peak time and £350–450 for other times. A few radio stations are also taking commercial ads. Guangzhou is the forerunner. It charges £30 for 10 seconds on its first channel and £25 for 10 seconds on its second channel.

The range of possible advertising is very wide: from billboards to television in trains to sponsored sports to videocassettes. Television in trains is provided on the express trains from Guangzhou to Hong Kong. The agent is Robert Chua in Hong Kong. The first sponsored sports event in China was a tennis match on 5 November 1979 between Bjorn Borg and John Alexander, in the Scandinavia Bank Challenge Trophy, followed by a match between Xu Meilin and Sun Chunlai of China. The sponsors were the Scandinavia Bank, Cathay Pacific, Marlboro Cigarettes, Seven-Up, and Titus Watches. The match was promoted by International Management of Hong Kong and Montpelier International Products. It was held in Guangzhou during the 1979 Autumn Fair. A second sponsored tennis match, organized by Philip Morris Association Inc., was held in Guangzhou in 1980.

Videocassettes are being used by a Hong Kong company called International Trade and Technology Research Associates (INTTRA). Since July 1979 INTTRA has had the rights to act as the sole representative of the China National Publications Import Corporation, through the CNPIC's National Video Advertising Services Division. INTTRA's idea is simple. It is based, like so many of the innovative ideas in Chinese marketing, on access to the end user. INTTRA provides a central showroom (typically in a ministry in Beijing) and regional showrooms in which it shows a videocassette of a company's products or services. It will also show the cassette in factories or on site. The cost of the basic service is $9000 for six months.

# Chapter 8

# The Trade in Media Products

The "energetic expansion of foreign trade, the importation of advanced technology, and the use of funds from abroad" was one of the "major policies" adopted at the second session of the Fifth National People's Congress in June 1980.

The senior state body for trade is the Ministry of Foreign Trade. The ministry works closely with the State Planning Commission and with the Financial and Economic Commission, which was set up in July 1979 and looks set to become extremely influential. These organizations are concerned with the strategy of economic and financial planning. They do not usually involve themselves with the details of trade, except that the ministry does negotiate directly with other governments for intergovernmental trade agreements. Also important is the China Council for the Promotion of International Trade (CCPIT), which was set up in 1952 to promote economic relationships between China and other countries. Its brief is both economic (to promote trade) and cultural (to increase understanding). It has a liaison office to arrange delegation visits, fairs, and so on (including the participation of Chinese people in foreign events); a department for exhibitions abroad; a department of technical exchange; a center for brochures and samples of foreign products; a department for publicity; and so forth. The council has recently shown itself to be very willing to consider all kinds of arrangements and deals.

In China, the pivotal organizations for exports and imports are the national trade corporations. They are usually called the China National [product] Import/Export Corporations, and usually abbreviated to CN [product] I/E Corporation or to their telegraphic address (e.g., INDUSTRY, etc.). They act as agencies for buying and selling.

Media products were being handled by several corporations at the end of 1979. Most light industrial products are handled by the CN Light Industrial Products Import/Export Corporation (known as INDUSTRY). It deals with TV and radio sets, studio equipment, and cinematographic equipment and supplies. Printing machinery is handled by the CN Machinery and Equipment Export Corporation (known as EQUIPEX). Printing ink is handled by the CN Chemicals Import/Export Corporation (known as SINOCHEM).

Books and periodicals are exported by Guozi Shudian, which also handles records, greeting cards, postcards, pictures, and so on. They are imported by the CN Publications Import Corporation (known as Senpikcorp).

Telecommunications equipment is handled by the CN Machinery I/E Corporation (known as MACHIMPEX).

This corporation also handles some optical equipment.

Since mid-1979, a range of electronic equipment including TV studio and transmission equipment, general broadcasting equipment, and telecommunications equipment has also been handled by a new corporation, the CN Instruments I/E Corporation. It is a measure of the confusion in China trade since 1978 that although the corporation's representative attended the 1979 autumn Guangzhou Fair, the corporation was not listed in the fair's guide, and many officials of associated corporations did not know of its existence.

Films are handled by the China Film Corporation. So far, the CFC has retained exclusive control of both exports and imports.

Since 1978 there has been a gradual but irreversible change in the role of the national trade corporations. The corporations have dominated China's foreign trade for a long time. They have always been tightly controlled by Beijing and been highly bureaucratic. Their proximity to the central economic authorities remains their strength, but it has also become their weakness. As China becomes more active, more expansionist, and as Beijing delegates more power to provinces and to individual factories, the monolithic trade corporations are losing some of their status and their importance.

The corporations' customers within China, the end users, are now asserting their part in the negotiating process. If a printer in Xi'an requires, say, a special thin ink for a fast-running rotary press, and this ink is unavailable locally, he or she is obliged to contact the nearest branch of SINOCHEM, which is hundreds of miles away in Shanghai. SINOCHEM then investigates the possibility of some China-made product and, if it is not possible, checks whether the purchase of this kind of ink complies with the current economic plans and, on a practical point, whether there is sufficient foreign currency. Only then does the corporation start the process of negotiating with foreign suppliers, which might take some time and would probably involve both buyer and seller in technical discussions without the presence or even any contribution from the printer.

The end user has been encouraged to take a more active role in foreign trading as part of Beijing's new policy to delegate more authority to the provinces and even to individual organizations. Users are encouraged to monitor foreign trends and to subscribe to foreign journals. Also, it is now possible for an organization that has earned foreign currency by exporting to keep the foreign currency and to decide when and how to spend it (previously, all foreign currencies were remitted to the capital). Many users have formed user-related groups that hold seminars and organize delegations to foreign countries. These user groups should be a priority target for foreign traders.

The triangle relationship between the trade corporation, the end user, and the foreign importer/exporter is extremely fluid. There are many stories of foreigners having continuing frustrations and difficulties in identifying the correct person to deal with. Sometimes the trade corporation insists on being involved in negotiations up to the contract, even if only as a witness; sometimes not. The best advice in these circumstances is that foreign traders should start as soon as possible to meet and know their Chinese opposite numbers. The first visit (say, a week at the Guangzhou Fair) may be puzzling and apparently pointless. But it will actually be enormously educational. And the Chinese will welcome back the visitor on his or her second visit, even if no contracts have been signed.

An example will illustrate the kind of confusion that is becoming all too typical. Many factories make TV sets for domestic sales. Some factories also assemble TV sets from imported components, sometimes for compensatory exports, sometimes for the domestic market. Also, TV sets are imported from Japan, Singapore, and so forth.

The traditional agent for TV sets is the China National Light Industrial Import/Export Corporation. For years, INDUSTRY has had a monopoly on the trade of TV sets. In late 1979, however, INDUSTRY faced a user's group that was fast becoming a rival. Its name was the China Precision Machinery Corporation.

The members of the China Precision Machinery Corporation had formed their new group because they were dissatisfied with the China National Machinery Import/Export Corporation (MACHIMPEX), to which they were affiliated, not with INDUSTRY. However, some of the members produce, as well as (heavy) machinery, TV sets, which are normally handled by INDUSTRY; film equipment, also handled by INDUSTRY; and even printing presses, which are handled by EQUIPEX. At the 1979 autumn Guangzhou Fair, the representatives of the China Precision Machinery Corporation were acting as agents for all these products. But so were the official trade corporations. Obviously, the negotiation of successful and binding contracts in these circumstances requires skill and luck.

The Guangzhou Fair (formally, the Chinese Export Commodities Fair) is changing rapidly due to these pressures. The fair had been held every spring and autumn, for a month at a time, since 1957. The Chinese trade corporations display their products and, in literally hundreds of rooms and in corridors, Chinese and foreigners negotiate contracts. By all accounts the Guangzhou Fair of spring 1979 was practically unworkable because of the numbers of foreign visitors and the confusion over which Chinese organization was responsible for which products and then over which organization had the authority to sign a contract and arrange finance. There were many stories of foreigners with hotel reservations who were unable to find a bed anywhere in the first two nights; and stories, too, of executives returning home with what they thought was a firm contract only to discover later that for some reason it was invalid. As a result, the Chinese have restructured the various procedures for foreign trade. As of spring 1980, most of the work previously done solely at the Guangzhou Fair is being done either at a new permanent Guangzhou trade exhibition or outside Guangzhou altogether. The fair continues to be held, but on a much smaller scale. The new policy gives much more power to the provincial authorities and to the end user.

The main trend at the national level is the development of joint ventures and compensatory trade. A joint venture is a financial arrangement (usually for manufacturing) in which the equity is held both by Chinese and foreign owners, and dividends can be remitted to the foreigner's own territory. Compensatory trade is an arrangement whereby the foreign company recovers its investment in the form of exports to its own territory. Obviously, the same operation can be a joint venture with elements of compensatory trade.

The law on joint ventures was announced, along with six other laws on crime and civil rights, at the second session of the Fifth People's National Congress in June 1979. Joint ventures are very attractive to foreign companies, which can exploit China's low labor costs to make goods both for the vast domestic market and for export. Typically, the foreign company supplies a proportion of the finance and most of the equipment.

# Chapter 9

# The Future

It is the fate of China today that all its actions, policies, and incidents, however small, are exposed to a world avid for information about the struggle of one of the oldest civilizations, now containing one-quarter of the world's population, to modernize itself. Facts on China's politics and economy may be scarce, but opinions and evaluations proliferate.

In the four years since the death of Mao Tsetung and the rise of Hua and Deng, China has changed more profoundly than probably any other nation. It is tempting to use the history of those three or four years to predict China's path in the eighties. Yet the recent changes probably owe more to the specific circumstances and tactics of those years than to any underlying principles and strategies. The remark of a leader-writer in the London *Times* (16 April

1980) that China is the world's longest lived and most successful totalitarian state is a useful corrective.

The basic issue facing the Chinese is the strength of the stability and openness of the new regime. Will it last? Will China rapidly pursue the four modernizations? Or will the immense strains of change bring a reaction against change?

The political mood in China at the beginning of the eighties is as volatile as it had been in 1976, as can be seen from the continuing shifts among the leadership. It was probably true to say, as many did in 1980, that Hua Guofeng was never more than a temporary leader; he had neither an established constituency to provide a historical base for his power nor the skill to exploit the new situation. But it is equally true that in 1976 many people fervently hoped he would provide stability, if not permanence. At the time of writing, it appears that his influence is fast diminishing, but it is hazardous to predict even a year ahead.

But several trends are apparent. The dictum "Learn truth from facts" has become widely accepted, and the "whateverists," so-named because they wish to follow "whatever" Mao said, have been eclipsed. Deng Xiaoping's own vivid slogan has become famous: "It doesn't matter whether the cat is white or black so long as it catches mice." Typical of this new approach was the announcement in *Shanxi Ribao* (and later everywhere else) that the famed Dazhai production brigade in north China, which since the 1950s had been spoken of with respect if not awe, should not serve as a model for other brigades without careful consideration. For years, Dazhai was supposed to be perfect, and its policies and activities were religiously copied by other brigades not only in Shanxi but throughout China (at least, the party ordered them to be copied). Of course, the dogma was too strict. Ideas and methods that genuinely worked in one place did not necessarily transfer very well to other places with different traditions, climate, and terrain. As *Shanxi Ribao* admitted, "How could a model of construction in mountainous areas serve as an example for the entire country to follow?" The *Beijing Review* (11 August 1980) made its own apology: "Owing to the influence of the erroneous line and the lack of on-the-spot investigation we described Dazhai as an advanced model in every respect. This is wrong, for which we should make a self-criticism." The new line was backed by Wang Renzhong, the influential head of the CCP Propaganda Committee, at a conference on TV and radio held in Beijing in October 1980. He said that "the media should tell the facts and speak the truth. . . . History has taught us lessons."

A second and linked trend is the increasing professionalism found at all levels and in both state and party sectors. The deaths of Mao and Zhou removed two great obstacles to change: (1) the admitted mess of the previous decades could now be cleared away (2) the stultifying rigidity and totalitarianism could be broken up. The provinces and republics could act independently of Beijing. Factories and other enterprises could practice self-management, setting their own production targets, fixing prices, and keeping a share of the profits (usually about 40 percent). Professional people in broadcasting and film could form professional organizations and formulate policy on the basis of professionalism, not ideology.

The exclusion of the bureaucrat in favor of the professional and the expert went against centuries of China's centralized, dictatorial, imperial rule. The change was not easy. But it was accepted as necessary in the cause of modernization. The scale of the dangers of using old methods to cope with new technologies was vividly demonstrated when a Japanese-imported oil rig collapsed, killing scores of workers, simply because the workers had not bothered to translate the safety manual. Afterwards, the minister of petroleum resigned.

The role of art in this new environment is a controversial topic, as might be expected. Some indication of the new drift can be gained from the speeches given at a forum attended by directors, writers, dramatists, and artists in Beijing in September; they were reprinted in *Renmin Ribao* on 4 October 1980:

> Huang Zongjiang, a scenarist of the August First Film Studio, said that bureaucracy in the field of literature and art should not be tolerated. Lan Guang, deputy director of the China Experimental Modern Drama Theater, stressed that as in the economic field, reforms should also be carried out in the field of literature and art. Lu Jun, editor-in-chief of the magazine *Dianying Chuangzuo* ("Script Writing") proposed that a law be enacted, defining the rights and interests of the writers and artists ensuring the implementation of the policy "Let a hundred flowers blossom and a hundred schools of thought contend."
>
> Lin Shan, a member of the Chinese Film Artists' Association, reviewed what had happened over the past 30 years, noting how literature and art flourished when the policy "Let a hundred flowers blossom and a hundred schools of thought contend" was upheld and how literature and art ceased to make progress when that policy was undetermined. Gu Yuan, deputy president of the Central Institute of Fine Arts, spoke against manifestations of commercialism prevailing in the literary and art circles at present. For instance, because traditional Chinese painting are a good export item, they are favored and encouraged to the neglect of other art forms. Other speakers attached importance to the improvement of the style of leadership and demanded that leading cadres in the field of literature and art learn from the late Premier Zhou Enlai, go among the literary and art workers, watch their per-

formances, have heart-to-heart talks with them, and get a clear understanding of their creative activities. This discussion is still going on.

This discussion has probably lasted without a break for a longer time in China than in any other country. The Chinese would be the first to admit that they are far from finding agreement on a solution.

# Appendix A

## A Chronology 1900−1980

**1900**

In the nineteenth century, the Qing dynasty became critically inefficient and vulnerable. Europeans and Americans captured increasing numbers of ports and territories; the era was characterized by the Opium War (1839−1842), the Anglo-French occupation of Beijing in 1856, and Russian and Japanese invasions (Sino-Japanese War, 1894−1895). The Qing was also attacked from within, e.g., the Taiping Revolution (1850−1864). The Yihetuan (Boxer Rising, 1900) was a xenophic reaction.

**1911**

A rebellion in Wuchang stimulated a countrywide revolution. The central imperial government collapsed. Diverse groups (republicans, warlords, traders) tried to assert their authority.

**1912**

The Guomintang (Nationalists) declared the founding of the Republic of China. Sun Yexian was proclaimed president but after a few months gave way to Hong Xiuquan who held power until his death in 1916. There was intense fighting between the Guomintang and other groups. In 1914, on the excuse of the outbreak of war in Europe, Japan invaded China and forced substantial concessions (1915).

**1919**

The 4 May Movement, a revolutionary nationalist uprising, protested the unfair conditions of the Versailles Treaty. This important, long-lived movement heralded the arrival of Marxist-Leninist ideology as a key source of revolution in China.

**1921**

The Chinese Communist Party was founded (1 July). During the 1920s the Guomintang (led again by Sun until his death in 1925) and the CCP (led by Mao Tsetung and others) alternatively collaborated and divided.

**1926**

The Northern (Expeditionary) Wars. From Guangzhou in the south Chiang Kaishek led the Guomintang, and some CCP forces, against several northern warlords; the USSR provided some assistance. The Guomintang were successful and quickly occupied central China.

In 1927 Chiang turned on the communists with surprise attacks, first in Shanghai (the Shanghai coup) and later in other cities. The communists retreated to the countryside. In 1928 Chiang led the Second Northern Expeditionary War and captured Beijing. For the first time since 1911 China had a semblance of a stable, united regime; but the CCP were excluded.

**1929**

Mao Tsetung and the CCP set up a "soviet" government in southern Jianxi and developed Mao's ideas of a rural-based communist society. The Jiangxi soviet, involving several million people, flourished during 1929–1934.

**1931**

The Japanese invaded Manchuria and attacked Shanghai and, in 1932, set up a "puppet" state in Manchuria under the Emperor Pu Yi of the Qing dynasty.

**1934**

The Long March: repeated Guomintang attacks forced Mao to move the CCP base from Jiangxi first to the west and then to the north to Yanan in northern Shaanxi. The Long March lasted 12 months and covered 6000 miles. En route, the CCP held a meeting at Zunyi, in Guizhou, which confirmed Mao's leadership and the principle of a mass, peasant-based party.

**1937**

The Sino-Japanese War, 1937–1945. The Guomintang and CCP nominally united to repel the Japanese; however, the Guomintang remained as the sole "official" state government. The CCP gained increasing credibility in the countryside for its guerrilla activities. Shanghai fell to the Japanese in 1937 and by the early 1940s the Japanese controlled all cities in the east of the country.

**1942**

The Yanan forum on literature and art (May) laid down the foundation of Maoist prescriptions for Chinese culture. The brunt was that political criteria took precedence over artistic criteria and that art could transcend class but must serve the workers and peasants.

**1945**

After the end of the Second World War and the Sino-Japanese War, the Guomintang and CCP fought against each other for the former Japanese territories.

**1949**

Liberation: the CCP defeated the Guomintang and established a strong, countrywide government with ambitious plans for reform. The People's Republic of China was founded (October). For the first few years the new republic was largely involved in the Korean War (1950–1953) and in a series of tough, disciplined mass movements (Three Antis, Five Antis) against revisionism, corruption, and other ideological 'errors.'

**1950**

In 1950 the Sino-Soviet Treaty of Friendship and Mutual Aid led to the first Five Year Plan (1953–1958).

**1956**

The Hundred Flowers campaign: Mao let "a hundred flowers bloom, a hundred schools of thought contend." The liberalization went too far for Mao's liking; in May 1957 he started the Anti-Rightist Movements.

**1958**

The Great Leap Forward: an ambitious state plan announced in February for tremendous increases in industrial production. The Commune Movement (May) was the equivalent in agriculture. The Great Leap saw some substantial increases, but at considerable costs. The communes suffered from bad management and terrible harvests. 1959 Mao gave up state chairmanship in favor of Liu Shaoqi. Liu remained chairman of PRC until his death in 1969, and dominated China until the Cultural Revolution.

**1960**

The USSR withdrew all personnel and assistance.

**1966**

The Cultural Revolution: a major conflict between the moderates, led by Liu Shaoqi, head of state, and the radicals, led by Mao Tsetung, chairman of the party. It started with the moderates attacking Mao and the Great Leap in a series of literary allegories from 1961 onwards. In 1965, Mao left Beijing to join his wife Jiang Qing in Shanghai. By July 1966, Lin Biao, in support of Mao, had secured Beijing, whence Mao returned to inaugurate the Cultural Revolution officially and to create the Red Guards. Fighting continued through 1966 to 1968. Liu Shaoqi was deprived of virtually all his posts in 1968 and called "a renegade, traitor, and scab." He died the following year. Lin Biao became Mao's acknowledged successor.

**1970**

At the 1970 Lushan Conference, Lin failed to be elected chairman of the PRC and attempted a coup against Mao. But he was discovered and, apparently, fled to the USSR in a plane which crashed in Mongolia. After his death his name was continually attacked and both he and (later) the Gang of Four were criticized for misleading Mao.

**1971**

China became a member of the United Nations. A U.S. Ping-Pong team visited China (April) and was followed, secretly, by Henry Kissinger in July.

**1972**

Richard Nixon visited Beijing (February). The Anti-Confucian Campaign, a complicated, partly radical movement against Lin Biao, grew during 1972 to 1974.

**1973**

The shift towards moderation continued. Deng Xiaoping, purged in 1967, became a deputy premier. The All-China Federation of Trade Unions, dissolved in the Cultural Revolution, was revived. Both Deng and Zhou Enlai (who is Deng's protector) pushed for economic and technological development over ideological discussion. They preferred people who were capable ("expert") over those who were politically pure ("red").

**1976**

The climacteric year, dominated by the deaths of Zhou Enlai and Mao Tsetung. Zhou had been premier since the Liberation and had popular support at all levels of the state and party. The eight months between his death and Mao's death saw continual power struggles between the triangle of Deng Xiaoping, the Gang of Four (backed by Mao), and Hua Guofeng.

Zhou died on 8 January. After a month Hua was appointed acting premier. In early April the riots in Tienanmen, Beijing, demonstrated popular support for Zhou and Deng. But, in reaction, the Gang of Four and Hua appeared to be stronger. On 7 April Hua was elevated to first vice chairman of the party (Mao was chairman) and premier of the state council. At the same meeting, having discussed Deng Xiaoping's "latest behavior" (i.e., the riots) and on the proposal of Mao, the party dismissed Deng from all his posts.

On 9 September, Mao died. Hua consolidated his position and arrested the Gang of Four (October).

**1977**

The moderates maintained control of both state and party. In July the Central Committee met. Hua was confirmed as chairman of the CCP and Deng was rehabilitated and appointed deputy premier and chief of the general staff of the PLA.

The eleventh CCP National Party Congress (August) confirmed the Central Committee's decisions.

## 1978

Liberalization continued. The China People's Political Consultative Conference (CPPCC), an assembly of communist and noncommunist parties and groups, met in February for the first time since 1964. The Fifth National People's Congress (NPC) held its first session (February); Deng was elected chairman. The NPC adopted the new constitution and announced a massive program of modernization.

Democracy Wall (on Changan Avenue) was officially acknowledged as a suitable place for posters, *dazibao* (November).

The PRC stopped its regular shelling of Taiwan's islands (December).

## 1979

In January numerous private newspapers appeared in Beijing and flourished. But in March Deng himself organized and tightened the regulations. Wei Jingsheng, editor of *Explorations*, was arrested. Later (October) he was found guilty of trying to disrupt and subvert the system and sentenced to 15 years imprisonment.

At the NPC's second session (June) Hua announced a modified policy of "readjusting, restructuring, consolidating, and improving the national economy." Also, Peng Zhen announced seven draft laws, some electoral laws, some criminal laws, and a law on international joint ventures (promulgated 1 January 1980).

The PRC celebrated its thirtieth anniversary (October).

The Fourth Writers and Artists Congress, the first for 19 years, was held in Beijing (October–November).

Retail prices of eight major foodstuffs were increased by 30 percent (November).

## 1980

The Eleventh Central Committee of the CCP held its fifth plenary session (February).

Zhao Ziyang and Hu Yaobang were elected to the Standing Committee of the politburo. Liu Shaoqi, the former prime minister, who was deposed by the Central Committee in 1968, was "completely rehabilitated." The Central Committee also confirmed the move to delete article 45 of the constitution, which gave citizens the right to "speak out freely, air their views fully, hold great debates, and write big-character posters" (the four freedoms, or "sida").

On May 17 an enormous memorial meeting, held in the Great Hall of the People, Beijing, and attended by 10,000 people, celebrated the final rehabilitation of Liu Shaoqi, and the end to "the biggest frame-up in our party's history."

The next day China successfully launched its first carrier rocket. As planned, the rocket came down between the Solomon Islands and Tuvalu.

The Fifth National People's Congress (NPC), the supreme state authority, held its third session from 30 August to 10 September. Hua Guofeng resigned as state premier and was replaced by Zhao Ziyang. Deng Xiaoping and other vice premiers also resigned; but Deng stayed as vice chairman of the party. The principle of self-management was fully endorsed. Income tax was levied on incomes over 800 yuan a month (it starts at 5 percent and rises to a ceiling of 45 percent). Further taxes were announced for join ventures: a 30 percent national tax and a 10 percent local tax on assessments which mean a total of 33 percent, with exemptions in the venture's early years. A 106-strong committee was set up to review the constitution. Plans were announced for a 10-year economic plan (1981–1990) and the sixth Five Year Plan (1981–1985). A new Nationality Law forbids dual nationality (aimed at overseas Chinese). The Marriage Law raises the age for marriage from 20 to 22 for men and from 18 to 20 for women; divorce is to be permitted.

The tenth National Broadcasting Conference opened in Beijing. The 200 delegates took stock of television and radio over the past 30 years.

The USA and China signed a massive wheat deal of 6–9 million tons in each of the next four years at a cost of £400 million a year (5 percent of China's current import bill). The U.S. wheat would have gone to the USSR but for the USA's post-Afghanistan boycott of Russia. Jiang Qing and the rest of the Gang of Four, and five others (collectively described as the Lin Biao Clique) were put on trial in November. They faced a total of 28 indictments, including treason and murder.

**1981**

In the New Year a more independent and aggressive policy by CCTV in its news bulletins resulted in several news items that were critical of senior officials (one short item on corruption included a film of senior cadres travelling in official limousines to shop at Beijing's biggest store), creating a national controversy and a public inquiry.

In January the sale by the Dutch government of submarines to Taiwan led to top-level protests in Beijing and eventually the reduction of diplomatic relationships from ambassador level to charge d'affaire level. The USA was also criticized for its leanings towards Taiwan.

On 25 January Jiang Qing and Zhang Chunqiao were

sentenced to death, with a two-year reprieve; Wang Hong-wen to life imprisonment; Yao Wengyuan to 20 years imprisonment, and the others to 16–20 years in prison.

During the spring the new U.S. administration headed by President Reagan was increasingly criticized by Beijing for its continuing friendship towards Taiwan, even though Reagan had softened his policy since the election campaign when he had occasionally talked of the "two Chinas," as if China and Taiwan were separate states. Chinese sensitivities were not helped by hearings held by the House of Representatives' Foreign Affairs Sub-Committee on Asia and the Pacific into the Taiwan issue. Several statements were made in favor of increasing U.S.–Taiwan trade, and of using Taiwan as a demonstration of U.S.-sponsored affluence. However, the visit of Alexander Haig, U.S. Secretary of State, to Beijing on 14–17 June, appeared to lay these fears to rest. It seemed that U.S. hostility towards the USSR more than compensated for its weakness on Taiwan.

Towards the end of June there were persistent rumors that Hua Guofeng had failed to achieved a satisfactory compromise on his future and that he would be demoted from all his significant titles.

# Appendix B

## A Note on the Language

It is difficult to learn Chinese. However, it is not too difficult to understand the structure of the language and even the barest knowledge can be very rewarding.

Written Chinese has evolved over thousands of years from pictograms and ideograms into a number of characters. About 5000 characters are commonly used, while a knowledge of 3000 is sufficient for most purposes. The characters are classified by their radical, the name given to one of a group of strokes. There are 214 radicals.

Traditional Chinese script has the great advantage of being uniform throughout China. However, the PRC's attempts to simplify the language have not been supported by the 'overseas' Chinese in Hong Kong and elsewhere. While the PRC Chinese are moving towards simplified characters, the overseas Chinese continue to use the traditional characters. So, two sets of characters are evolving. This difference becomes important when one is considering the translation or printing of Chinese, or the distribution of Chinese-language texts.

Spoken Chinese has always differed widely in different areas. Each region has evolved its own sounds (phonemes) to represent the various characters. It is this representation of meaning by sound that makes Chinese uniquely difficult. Chinese does not have a phonetic alphabet; instead it has (seven) strokes which are used to form characters. The point is that the strokes, unlike the letters in an alphabet, have no equivalent intrinsic sound. In fact, it is seldom possible to look at a character and deduce either its sound or its meaning. With a phonetic alphabet, one can look at the word *magisterial* for the first time, and know roughly how it is pronounced and even its meaning. In Chinese, neither deduction may be possible.

Each dialect has a range of different sounds. The standard sound system is the Beijing dialect (the old Mandarin) which is now called putonghua. Putonghua has about 400 sounds with which to convey the meanings of all the characters. Put another way, each sound has to convey 10 common characters and about 20 unusual ones. The Chinese do have ways of dispelling some of the confusion. First they use tones. (It is the energetic use of tones that gives Chinese its well-known sing-song sound.) Putonghua has four tones. The first tone is level, the second is rising, the third falls and rises, and the fourth falls. For instance: *shu* means *book, shu* means *ripe, shu* means to *count*, and *shu* means *tree*. The scope for confusion is vast. *Mài* means *to sell, mai* means *to buy.*

The second device is to use two sounds in harness that indicate approximately the same meaning. *Yi* means *clothing*, but it also means a dozen other things. *Lu* also means *clothing*, and a dozen other things. So the Chinese might say *yilu* to make doubly certain. But confusion is ripe; and the Chinese love puns.

Many attempts have been made by foreigners to construct an ersatz phonetic alphabet that could be used to "romanize" Chinese sounds. The most widespread is the Wade-Giles system. However, in 1958, the PRC adopted its own *pinyin* system (the word means "phonetic"). No phonetic system is perfect, but pinyin is remarkably good. Its widespread use would benefit both Chinese and foreigners enormously.

This survey uses pinyin with a few exceptions. It has kept the Wade-Giles spelling of Tibet (Xizang), and of Mao Tsetung (Mao Zedong). It has also kept the old European name for China instead of substituting the more accurate, but quite different, "Zhongguo."

In pronunciation, whether from the base of Wade-Giles or pinyin, the foreigner should try to emulate the emphatic tones and sounds of the Chinese. All syllables are stressed (Marx becomes Ma Ke Se) and all are stressed equally.

Another point is that in pinyin, but not in Wade-Giles, the syllables are written as one word. For instance, Hua Kuo Feng is Wade-Giles; Hua Guo Feng is incorrect pinyin; Hua Guofeng is correct. Likewise, Dong An Men Street is better as Donganmen Street, and it really should be Dongmen Dajie. See table B.1.

**Table B.1**    Pronunciation

| Initials | |
| --- | --- |
| The sound represented in pinyin by the letter | is pronounced like the English |
| b | bill |
| p | pike[1] |
| m | mad |
| f | fall |
| d | dull |
| t | talk[1] |
| n | nose |
| l | last |
| g | go |
| k | cold[1] |
| h | hand |
| z | needs |
| c | czar[1] |
| s | sell |
| zh | jug |
| ch | church[1] |
| sh | show |
| r | pleasure |
| j | jeep |
| q | cheese[1] |
| x | she |

[1] Strongly aspirated

**Table B.2**  Pronunciation

|  | Finals |
| --- | --- |
| The sound represented in pinyin by the letter | is pronounced like the English |
| a | father |
| ai | like |
| an | man |
| ang | longer |
| ao | out |
| c | cup |
| ci | lake |
| en | given |
| eng | lung |
| i (yi) | see |
| ia (ya) | tar |
| ian (yan) | cayenne |
| iang (yang) | young |
| iao (yao) | yowl |
| ie (ye) | yes |
| iu (you) | yoke |
| in (yin) | keen |
| ing (ying) | sing |
| iong (yong) | "Jungfrau" |
| o | stop |
| ong | song |
| ou | coat |
| u (wu) | moon |
| u, $u^2$(yu) | rue |

[2] after j, q, x, and y

# Appendix C

# Population

The population of China at the end of 1979 was 970,000,000, according to the *Communique on the Fulfilment of China's 1979 National Economic Plan*, issued by the State Statistical Bureau (SSB) on 30 April 1980. The figure for the end of 1978 had been 958,090,000; an increase of 12,830,000 people (same source). These figures may include Taiwan; the SSB communique in *Xinhua's* bulletin says they do, but *Beijing Review* says they do not.

These figures are based on data gathered in a variety of ways and may be inaccurate. China last held a census in 1964. It plans a more elaborate census in 1981. Meanwhile, it is currently starting a major project with the UN Fund for Population Activities (485 Lexington Avenue, New York, NY 10017) which may soon be able to give continuously accurate figures.

The target for the year 2000 is to strive to limit the population to 1200 million, according to Hua Guofeng in 1980 (at the third session of the Fifth National People's Congress). Hua said the State Council proposed a "crash drive" for parents to have only one child. He said that the population had grown too quickly, with 630 million people (65 percent of the total) under 30 years old. Many of these people were capable of having children.

# Appendix D

## Names and Addresses of Selected Media Organizations

This list contains the addresses of the main organizations mentioned in the text. In practice, the Chinese Post Office will deliver any mail that has the name of the organization and the city. Streets and street numbers are provided here for the benefit of visitors.

### GOVERNMENT AND CCP ORGANIZATIONS

Ministry of Foreign Affairs
225 Chaoyangmennei Dajie, Beijing
Tel: 55 5831

Ministry of Communications
Beijing
Tel: 864 2021

Ministry of Culture
Beijing
Tel: 44 2131
The Film Bureau's telephone is: 44 1316

Ministry of Posts and Telecommunications
Xi Changan Jie, Beijing
Tel: 66 1250, 66 0540 Cables: MINPOSTEL

Ministry of Education
35 Damucang Huton, Beijing
Tel: 66 8421

Central Committee, CCP
Beijing
Tel: 66 1300

## BROADCASTING

The Central Broadcasting Administration

The Central Television Station

The Central People's Broadcasting Station

Radio International

The China Record Company

The Central Radio and TV Art Troupe

The Central Broadcasting Orchestra

The Broadcasting Institute

The Broadcasting Research Institute

Fuxingmenwai Dajie, Beijing
Tel: 86 2753, 8581

Beijing Television Station
14 Xinjie Koyai Dajie, Beijing
Tel: 66 7878

Beijing Radio
Fu Xinmen Zhenwu Miao, Beijing
Tel: 86 3045

Shanghai Television Station
651 Nanjing Xilu, Shanghai
Tel: 56 5899

Guangdon Television Station
Renmin Beilu, Guangdon
Tel: 30 030

## PRINT

China National Publications Import Corporation
PO Box 88, Beijing
Tel: 44 0731/0726 Cables: PUBLIM PEKING

Commercial Press
190 Tiantongau, Lu, Shanghai
Tel: 66 1217

Science and Technology Publishing House
450 Ruijing Erlu, Shanghai
Tel: 37 0160

Wen Wei Po
197-199 Wanchai Road, Hong Kong
Tel: 5-722211

## FILM

China Film Corporation
25 Xinwai Jie, Beijing
Tel: 66 7831/0116/7819 Cable: CFDCORP

China Film Equipment Corporation
25 Xinwai Jie, Beijing
Tel: 66 2204

Beijing Film Studios
Beitaipingzhuang, Beijing
Tel: 66 8441

China Film Archives
25 Xinwai Jie, Beijing
Tel: 66 2361

Central Newsreel and Documentary Film Studio
(i)  Beitaipingzhuang
(ii) 43 Xinjiejou, Beijing
Tel: 66 8861

Beijing Film Laboratory
Beitaipingzhuang
Tel: 66 6561

Beijing Film Institute
Beijiao, Beijing
Tel: 27 5631

Beijing Academy of Film
Beijiao, Beijing
Tel: 27 5631

August First Film Studios
Tel: 33 5434

China Film Workers Association
Beitaipingzhuang, Beijing
Tel: 66 8861

Chinese Cinematography Club (CCC)
Beijing
Tel: 55 6065

Science and Education Film Studios
Xinwai Jie
Tel: 66 6731

Agricultural Film Studios
Beijing

Tel: 89 1814

Educational Film Studios Laboratory
Guowai Jie, Beijing
Tel: 44 1318

Shanghai Film Studios
Chao Qi Beilu, Shanghai
Tel: 39 3811

Shanghai Animation Film Studios
Shanghai Dubbing Studio
Tel: 37 0608

Shanghai Science and Educational Film Studios
Tel: 38 9121

## TELECOMMUNICATIONS

Beijing Institute of Communications
Beijing
Tel: 668 1558

Central Post Office
Fuxingmennei Avenue, Beijing
Tel: 66 4900

Academy of Space Sciences
Beijing
Tel: 87 5040

National Academy of Space Technology
PO Box 2417, Beijing
Tel: 89 3042

## PUBLISHING

People's Publishing House
166 Chaoyangmennei Dajie, Beijing
Tel: 55 0501

Social Sciences Publishing House
6 Ritan Lu, Jianguomenwai, Beijing

Foreign Language Press
Beijing
Tel: 89 0231

Foreign Language Publishing House
Baiwanzhuang, Beijing
Tel: 89 1616

Beijing Publishing House
51 Dongxinglong Jie, Beijing
Tel: 75 4314

People's Fine Arts Publishing House
32 Bei Zongbu Hutong, Beijing
Tel: 55 0290

People's Literature Publishing House
166 Chaoyangmennei Dajie, Beijing

People's Music Publishing House
166 Chaoyangmennei Dajie, Beijing
Tel: 55 0385

Science Publishing House
137 Chanoyangmennei Dajie, Beijing
Tel: 598 2574

Xinhua Printing Works
3 Chegongzhuang, Beijing
Tel: 89 0361

Foreign Languages Printing Works
Erligou Xijiao, Beijing
Tel: 89 3218

People's Printing Works
Beijing
Tel: 33 3246

China Translation and Publishing Services
  Corporation
PO Box 1818, Beijing
Tel:  44 4625

# Bibliography

Anderson, Michael. "China's Great Leap Towards Madison Avenue." In *Journal of Communication*. Winter 1981.

Chen, Theodore H. E. *Thought Reform of the Chinese Intellectuals*. Hong Kong University, Hong Kong, 1960.

*Chiao tung kungpao* ("Gazette of Communication"). Nanking 1929–1937 and 1938–1948. Available from Center for Chinese Research Materials, Washington, D.C.

*China Directory*. Radiopress, 7 Kawada-cho, Ichigaya, Shinjuku-ku, Tokyo.

*China: A General Survey*. Foreign Language Press, Beijing, 1979.

*China Phone Book*. GPO Box 11581, Hong Kong.

*China*. Nagel's Encyclopaedia-Guide, Geneva, 1979.

Chu, Godwin, et al. *Communication and Development in China*. Communication Monograph, No 1, East-West Communication Institute, Honolulu, 1976.

Chu, Godwin C. *Popular Media in China: Shaping New Cultural Patterns*. University Press of Hawaii, Honolulu, 1978.

Chu, Godwin C, and Hsu, Francis. *Moving a Mountain: Cultural Change in China*. East-West Communication Institute, Honolulu, 1979.

Chu, Godwin C. *Radical Changes Through Communication in Mao's China*. University Press of Hawaii, Honolulu, 1977.

Dillon, Michael. *Dictionary of Chinese History*. Cass, London, 1979.

"Enemy of the People?" A transcript of the trial of Wei Jing-sheng. *Harpers & Queen*, London, April, May, June 1980.

Fang, Josephine. "Library Developments in the People's Republic of China." In *Annual of the Library and Book Trade*. Bowker, New York, 1976.

Goodman, David. *Beijing Street Voices*. Marion Boyars, London, 1981.

Roger Howard. *Contemporary Chinese Theatre*. Heinemann, London, 1978.

Howkins, John. *The 1980 China Media Industry Report*, Nord Media, London, 1980.

Howkins, John. "Chinese TV's Great Leap Forward." In *Broadcast*. London, 14 January 1980.

Hsia Yen. "History of Chinese Film and the Leadership of the Party." In *Renmin Ribao* ("People's Daily"). Beijing, 16 November, 1957.

Kaplan, Frederick, et al. *Encyclopaedia of China Today.* Macmillan, London, 1979.

Kuo, Thomas C. "State of Current Library Operations in China." In *Newsletter.* Center for Chinese Research Materials, Washington, D.C., April 1976.

Leys, Simon. *Broken Images.* Allison and Busby, London, 1979.

Liu, Allan. *Communications and National Integration in Communist China.* University of California Press, Berkeley, 1971.

Liu Tseng chi, "The Press in New China." In *Culture and Education in New China.* Foreign Language Press, Beijing, undated.

*Main Documents of the Second Session of the Fifth National People's Congress.* Foreign Language Press, Beijing, 1979.

McCormick, Robert. "Central Broadcasting and Television University." In *China Quarterly.* London, March 1980.

MacFarquhar, Roderick. "A Visit to the Chinese Press," In *China Quarterly.* London, January/March 1973.

Mei Tso. "The Chinese People's Broadcasting System." In *Culture and Education in New China.* Foreign Language Press, Beijing, undated.

Mirsky, Jonathan, et al. "China: Special Issue." In *Index on Censorship.* Writers and Scholars International, London, February 1980.

Needham, Joseph, et al. *Science and Civilisation in China.*

Cambridge University Press, in progress (several volumes already published).

Rawski, Thomas. *China's Transition to Industrialism*. Dawson, Folkestone, 1980.

Rayns, Tony, and Meek, Scott. *Electric Shadows: 45 Years of Chinese Cinema*. BFI Dossier No. 3, BFI, London, 1980.

Richter, Harald. *Publishing in the People's Republic of China*. Mitteilungen des Instituts für Asienkunde, Hamburg, 1978.

Ronan, Colin. *The Shorter Science and Civilisation in China*. Volumes 1 and 2. Cambridge University Press, Cambridge, 1978/1981.

Schramm, Wilbur, and Atwood, L. Edwin. *Circulation of Third World News: A Study of Asia*. Chinese University of Hong Kong, 1980.

Shue, Vivienne. "China: On the Wire." In *InterMedia*, International Institute of Communications, March 1980.

Terrill, Ross. *The Future of China: After Mao*. André Deutsch, London, 1979.

Ting Wang. *Chairman Hua*. Hurst, London, 1980.

Tregear, Thomas R. *China: A Geographical Survey*. Hodder & Stoughton, London, 1980.

Tso Hung. "Broadcasting in China." In *People's China*. Beijing, November 16, 1953.

Yu, Frederick T. C. *A Brief Report on the Home Service Broadcasts of the Central People's Broadcasting Stations in Beijing*. Available from University of Southern California, 1952.

Yu, Frederick. *Mass Persuasion in Communist China*. Praeger, New York, 1964.

Yu Liu. "The Party's Leadership and Struggle in China's Film Industry Before Liberation." In *Chungkuo Tienyin* ("Chinese Film"). Beijing, 1959, No. 6.

Wang, S. W. "Impressions of Chinese Libraries and the Chinese Book Market." In *Australian Academic and Research Libraries*. March 1974.

Wen Chi tse. "People's Broadcasting During the Last Ten Years." *Hsinhua Yuehpao* ("New China Monthly"). Beijing, October 1955.

*Will They Ever Buy Our Products*. JANSON Marketing, Kristinelundsgatan 5, 5-411 37 Goteborg, Sweden, 1980.

Wu Chi pu. "Fully Develop the Five Functions of a Provincial Newspaper." In *Hsinhua Penyuekhan* ("New China Fortnightly"). Beijing, February 25, 1959.

Wu, Eugene. "Recent Development in Chinese Book Publishing." In *China Quarterly*. London, January/March 1973.

# Index

Advertising, 107–12
  agencies, 108–9
  foreign, 108, 110
  media, 110–12
  poster, 108, 110
  purpose of, 107–8
  radio, 111
  television, 17, 30, 51, 108, 110
Agricultural Film Studios, 70
Agriculture, 8, 15–16, 18, 108
Albania, 59
Alexander, John, 111
All China Federation of Trade
  Unions, 86
American Broadcasting Co.
  (ABC), 31
American Institute of Aeronaut-
  ics and Astronautics, 3
Antze, 30
Asian Motion Picture Company,
  66
Asian-Pacific Broadcasting Union
  (ABU), 31
Audience
  estimating size of, 109–10
  film, 76–77
  television, 43–46, 50–51
August First Film Studios, 66, 70
Australia, 92

Bank of China, 5, 19
Beijing, 12–13, 18, 23
  bookstores, 91
  as broadcasting center, 25–26
  film in, 70, 71, 73, 75–76
  publishing in, 82–83, 84
  radio in, 53

telephone cable in, 97–98
  television in, 17, 27–29, 47–50
  trading corporations and,
    115–16
Beijing Advertising Corp., 108–9
Beijing Broadcasting Equipment
  Factory, 26
Beijing Film Studios, 70, 71, 73
Beijing No. 3 Radio and Television Parts Factory, 34
Beijing Opera, 11
Beijing Radio, 58–59
Beijing Review, 21, 33, 44,
    85–86, 91, 121
Beijing Television, 27–29, 47–50
  advertising on, 110–11
  organization, 49
  programming, 48–49
  university, 44, 49–50
"Bicycling," 27
Book(s)
  distribution, 91–93
  fair, 92
  printing, 88–90
  publishing, 80–85
  stores, 91–92
  trade in, 114
Borg, Bjorn, 111
British Broadcasting (BBC), 46,
    52
Broadcasting, 25–64
  center for, 25–26
  growth of, 31–32
  satellite, 103
  wired, 26
  see also Radio, Television
    Broadcasting Institute, 26

Broadcasting Research Institute, 26
Budget, national, 18–19

Canada, 78, 103
Canton, 27, 109
Cao Yu, 74–75
Cartographic Publishing House, 85
Central Broadcasting Administration (CBA), 25, 26, 42, 44, 46, 63, 101
Central Broadcasting Science Research Factory, 26
Central Committee CCP, 9, 25, 56, 83, 86, 96
Central News and Documentary Film Studios, 70
Central People's Broadcasting Station (CBPS), 26, 44–45, 52–58, 63
  organization, 56–57
  programming, 57–58
Central Radio and Television Art Troupe, 26
Changchun, 66, 70
Chen Chong, 78
Chengtu, 28, 35, 70, 110
China Central Television Station (CCTV), 26–29, 35–47, 49
  advertising on, 110
  programming, 35–44
  studios, 42–43
China Council for Promotion of International Trade (CCPIT), 114
China Difference, The, 2
China Equipment Corporation, 71
China Film Archives, 71
China Film Corporation (CFC), 68–69, 71, 74–78, 115
China Film Distribution and Exhibition Corporation, 69

China National (CN) Import/Export Corporations, 92–93, 114–17
China Precision Machinery Corporation, 117
China Reconstructs, 15
China Record Company, 26
China Television Service, 46–47
China Youth Publishing House, 85
Chinese Academy of Sciences, 98, 101
Chinese Advertising Company, 108–9
Chinese Communist Party (CCP), 8–10
  broadcasting policy, 25–26, 46, 54–56
  Central Committee, 9, 25, 56, 83, 96
  communications and, 4–5
  film industry and, 69, 73
  Propaganda Committee, 25, 56, 63, 83, 85, 121
  publishing and, 81–87
Chinese Photography Publications House, 84
Chinese Society of World Cinema, 69
Chinese Telegraph Administration, 95
Chu, Godwin, 5
Cinema. See Film
Commercial Press, 84, 88
Communications, passim
  Chinese attitude toward, 2, 5–6
  communism and, 1–6
  future of, 119–23
  media organizations, 141–47
  society and, 4
Communications Act (1934), 17
Consumer goods, 21–22
Corning Glass Works, 34

Corporations, national trade,
    114–17
Costa-Gavras, Constantin, 45
Couve de Murville, 2
Cultural Book Society, 81
Cultural Revolution, 7, 8–13, 23,
    107
  filmmaking during, 67
  publishing during, 82
  radio during, 59, 64
  television during, 28, 31, 44

Dazhai production brigade,
    120–21
Deng Xiaoping, 8–10, 12–16,
    22–24, 31, 55, 119–20
Department of Industry and
    Commerce, 96
Dialect, 135–36
  pronunciation guides, 137, 138
  as publishing problem, 79
  used on radio, 53–54, 56, 59
  used on television, 29
Ding Ling, 92
Dubbing Film Studio, 70–71

Earth station, 104–5
Economy, Chinese, 18–22
Education, 27, 44–45, 49, 57
Education Film Studios, 70
Electronics. *See*
    Telecommunications
Entertainment
  radio, 57–58
  television, 27, 45–46, 50
Equipment
  broadcasting, 115
  film, 72
  printing, 88–90
  telecommunications, 114–15
  television, 114–18
European Space Agency (ESA),
    101, 103

Fairs, book, 92
Family living standards, 21–22
Federal Communications Com-
    mission, 17
Fiber optics, 97–99
Fifth National People's Congress,
    15–19, 32, 58, 96, 118
Film, 65–78
  audiences, 76–77
  coproductions, 78
  Cultural Revolution and, 67
  distribution and exhibition,
    74–78
  equipment, 72
  fee structure for, 74–75
  history of, 66–67
  production, 67–68, 70–74
  projection teams, 75–76
  regulation of, 68–69
  subjects, 73–74, 77–78
  television, 43, 78–79
  theaters, 75–76
  trade in, 115
First August Radio, 55
Forbidden City, 13, 25
Foreign
  advertising, 108, 110–11
  broadcasts, 31
  currency, 116
  films, 68, 69
  language magazines, 87, 90–91
  perceptions of China, 2
  trade in media products,
    113–18
Foreign Language Press, 84
Four modernizations, the, 15–16,
    58, 108, 120
Fourth National Party Congress,
    9
France, 29, 45, 92, 102, 104

Gang of Four, 10–15, 22–24, 64,
    65, 67, 73, 97–98

*General Line of Socialist Construction,* 82
General Meteorological Bureau, 101
*Congren Ribao,* 86
Great Leap Forward, 7, 27, 66–67, 82
Green, Timothy, 28
Gu Mu, 15, 20
Guangzhou, 28, 29, 108–11
Guangzhou Fair, 115, 116–18
Guozi Shudian, 92, 114
Gutenberg, Johannes, 81

Han dynasty, 80, 95
Hangzhou, 21–22
He Zinzhi, 92
Hohhot Film Studios, 71
Hong Kong, 43, 44, 56, 66, 86, 109–11
Hope, Bob, 45
Hu Yaobang, 24
Hua Guofeng, 5, 8, 12–19, 22–24, 31, 32, 119–20
Hundred Flowers Awards, 77–78

Ideology, 5, 8–9, 14, 16
Illiteracy, 79
Imports
  film, 68, 69
  paper and printing, 90
  television equipment, 30, 33–35
  television programs, 45–46
Income Tax, 21
Industry, 15–16, 18–20, 108
Inflation, 22
Intellectuals, payments to, 74–75
Interdependence, world, 8
International Telecommunication Union (ITU), 102, 105
International Trade and Technical Research Association, 111–12
Isolation policy, 7–8

Ivens, Joris, 66

Japan, 4, 30, 33–35, 43, 52, 66, 68, 92, 102, 117
Jiang Qing, 8, 10–11, 24, 28, 67
*Jiefang Ribao,* 86

Lan Pin. *See* Jiang Qing
Language, 79–80, 134–36
  pronunciation guides, 137, 138
  *see also* Dialect
"Laughter of a Distressed Man," 65, 73
Law, communications, 17
Leader, Chinese concept of, 12
Li Lienching, 42
Li Rentang, 73, 78
Light Industry Research Institute of Paper Technology, 88
Lin Biao, 23, 73
Loudspeakers, wired broadcasts to, 26, 54, 55
Lumière brothers, 66

McCann, Erikson Matheson, 109
Macartney, Lord,
Magazines. *See* Periodicals
Malraux, André, 45
Mao Tsetung, 4, 8, 13, 16, 81, 119–20
  Cultural Revolution and, 7–13, 23–24
Marxism-Leninism, 16–17
Media
  advertising, 110–12
  future of, 119–23
  organizations, names and addresses of, 141–47
  products, trade in, 113–18
  *see also* individual media
Meng Guangjun, 69
Ministry of Commerce, 32
Ministry of Culture, 26, 68, 78, 83
Ministry of Education, 44

Ministry of Foreign Trade, 113
Ministry of Light Industries, 90
Ministry of Posts and Telecom-
    munications (PTT), 96, 101
Ministry of Telecommunications,
    30–31
Moderates, 9–10, 12–13
Modernization, 14
    advertising and, 107–8
    of filmmaking, 73
    four modernizations and,
        15–16, 108, 120
    future, 120–23
    of telecommunications, 99
    of television equipment, 33–35
    in totalitarian system, 6
Motion Pictures. *See* Film

National Academy of Space
    Technology (NAST), 99,
    101–2
    organization of, 101
National Aeronautics and Space
    Administration (NASA),
    101, 103
National Book Fair, 92
National Broadcasting Company
    (NBC), 45
National Bureau of the Radio
    and Television Body, 34
National defense, 15–16, 108
National Industrial Congress, 14
National People's Congress, 13
National Publications Import
    Corporation, 112
National Video Advertising Ser-
    vices, 112
Nationalists, 81
News programs
    radio, 57, 58–59, 63
    television, 27–28, 44, 50
Newspapers
    distribution of, 92
    national, 85–86
    regional, 86

Nixon, Richard, 99
Northern Shaanxi Xinhua Broad-
    casting Station, 54
Nuclear weaponry, 99

Omei Film Studios, 70

Pathé newsreels, 66
Pearl River Film Studios, 70
People's Education Publishing
    House, 85
People's Fine Arts Publishing
    House, 84
People's Liberation Army
    (PLO), 10, 14
People's Literature Publishing
    House, 84
People's Music Publishing House,
    84
People's Physical Culture Pub-
    lishing House, 85
People's Publishing House, 84
Periodicals
    distribution of, 92–93
    foreign, 90–91
    foreign language, 87
    printing, 88–91
    magazine, 86–87
trade in, 114
Politics in China, 7–24
    chronology of, 124–33
    consolidation years, 14–19
    in Cultural Revolution, 7,
        8–13, 23
    economy and, 18–22
    Gang of Four and, 10–15,
        23–24
    during Great Leap Forward, 7
    isolation, 7–8
    moderates vs. radicals in,
        9–10, 12–13
Population 1, 8, 139–40
Posters, wall, 5, 108
Printing, 79–93
    history, 80–83

State Publications Administration (SPA) and, 82, 83–85
techniques, 88–91
*see also* Publishing
Professionalism, 121–22
Projection teams, film, 75–76
Propaganda Committee CCP, 25, 56, 83, 85, 121
Publishing, 79–93
  book, 80–85
  distribution, 91–93
  expansion, 82
  history, 80–83
  periodical, 85–87

Qing dynasty, 2

Radicals, 9–10, 12–13
Radio, 52–64
  advertising, 111
  Beijing, 58–59
  Central People's Broadcasting Station and, 52–58
  Communist Party and, 54–56
  dialects used on, 53–54, 56, 59
  dissident, 55
  growth of, 31–32
  history of, 54–55
  programming, 53, 57–58, 60–62, 63
  Radio International, 59–64
  sets, 31–33, 55
  station levels, 52–53
  technology, 52
  university, 58
Radio Corporation of America (RCA), 99
Radio International, 26, 59–64
  organization, 63–64
  programming, 60–62, 63
Reading rooms, 91–92
*Red Flag*, 87
"Red" vs. "expert," 8–10
Remote sensing satellite, 104
Ren Yolin, 42

*Renmin Ribao*, 5, 85–86, 122
Robert Chua group, 109, 111
Russia. *See* Union of Soviet Socialist Republics

Sanlian Bookstore, 84
Satellite, communications, 59, 63, 99–105
  broadcasting, 103
  Earth station, 104–5
  orbits, 102–3
  program for, 100
  remote sensing, 104
  research center, 101–2
  technology, 97–105
Science Press, 84
Science and technology, 15–16, 108
Science and Technology Film Studios, 70
*Scientific American*, 90–91
Shanghai, 10–12, 46
  advertising in, 107–8
  bookstores in, 91
  film in, 66–67, 70–73, 75–76
  publishing in, 84
  radio in, 53
  telephone cable in, 98
  television in, 17, 27, 33, 50–52
Shanghai Advertising and Packaging Corporation, 107–8
Shanghai Film Studios, 66–67, 71–73
Shanghai 519 Factory, 98
Shanghai No. 1 Television Factory, 34
Shanghai Television Station, 50–52
  advertising on, 110–11
  organization, 51–52
  programming, 51
*Shanxi Ribao*, 120
Slogans, 14, 15, 120
Social Sciences Publishing House, 85

Society, communications and, 4
Song Hua Giang, 49
Space technology, 3, 99–105
State Planning Commission, 113
State Publications Administration
    (SPA), 82, 83–85
State Statistical Bureau, 22, 32,
    68, 76
Staunton, George, 2
Suzhou TV Component Factory,
    34

Taching, 14
Taiwan, 55, 56, 105
Technology, 8, 15–16
    future, 121–22
    importing, 18
    printing, 88–91
    radio, 52
    space, 3, 99–105
    telecommunications, 97–105,
        114–15
    television, 28–30, 33
Telephone system, 95–98
Television, 16–17, 26–52
    advertisements on, 17, 30, 51,
        108, 110–11
    audience, 43–46, 50–51
Beijing Television Station, 47–50
    CCTV, 35–47
    color, 17, 28–30, 34
    dialect used on, 29
    equipment, 29–30, 33–35
    films, 43, 78–79
    growth of, 31–32
    imported programs on, 31,
        45–46
    programming, 27, 35–44,
        48–49, 51
    by satellite, 101
    sets, 31–35
    Shanghai Television Station,
        50–52
    studios, 42–43
    technology, 28–30, 33

university, 44–45, 49–50
Theaters, motion picture, 75–76
Tianjin, 27, 28, 29, 30, 33
Tibet, 26, 59
Tibetan People's Broadcasting
    Station, 26
Tienanmen, 12–14, 25
Trade in media products, 113–18
    compensatory, 118
    confusion in 116–18
    corporations handling, 114–17
    joint ventures, 118
Tung Fang Hung, 99

Union of Soviet Socialist Republ-
    ics, 7, 29, 31, 46, 102
United Kingdom, 3–4, 29, 43,
    68, 92, 98
United Nations, 102
United States, 4, 17, 31, 45, 59,
    66, 68, 78, 92, 101, 103, 104
Universal Postal Union, 105

Visnews, 31, 44

Wages, 20–22
    for filmmakers, 74
Wall posters, 5, 108
Wang Binggian, 19
Wang Chen, 81
Wang Hongwen, 11
Wang Yang, 73
Wauwen Studios, 92
Wen Wei Po, 86, 109
Wenwei Bao, 78

West Germany, 29, 90, 92, 102,
    104
Western Union, 99
Wired broadcasting, 26, 54, 55
Writers, payments to, 74–75

Xi'an, 66, 70, 115
Xianyang, 33–34
Xie Bingxin, 92

Xinhua News Agency (XHNA), 11, 12, 32, 55, 57, 63, 86
Xinhua Printing Works, 79–82, 88–90
Xinhua Shudian, 91

Yanan Xinhua Broadcasting Station, 54
Yao Wenyuan, 11

Yu Qiuli, 96
Yugoslavia, 55, 68

Zhang Chunqiao, 11
Zhang, Kejia, 92
Zhao Dan, 67
Zhong Hua Publishing House, 84
*Zhongguo Qingnian Bao,* 86
Zhou Enlai, 8–10, 12–14, 120